Journey to
Tradition

Journey to Tradition

The Odyssey of a Born-Again Jew

by Michael Graubart Levin

Ktav Publishing House, Inc.
HOBOKEN, NEW JERSEY
1986

© 1986 MICHAEL GRAUBART LEVIN

Library of Congress Cataloging-in-Publication Data

Levin, Michael Graubart.
  Journey to tradition.

  Bibliography: p.
  1. Levin, Michael Graubart. 2. Jews—United States—
Biography. 3. Jews—Return to Orthodox Judaism.
I. Title.
E184.J5L5729   1985   296.8'32'0924   [B]   85-24083
ISBN 0-88125-093-7

MANUFACTURED IN THE UNITED STATES OF AMERICA

To My Family,

and to my Talmud Teacher,
Dr. Haim Agus, z.l.

Contents

Acknowledgments

My thanks are due first to Bernard Scharfstein, and to my editor at Ktav, Yaakov Elman, both of whom believed in this book's possibilities from the first. I could not ask for a better editor than Yaakov Elman. His sensitivity to language and to *Yiddishkeit* is evident on every page. Errors and inaccuracies in the text, of course, remain strictly the responsibility of the author.

Next, my thanks to those who read and commented on all or part of earlier drafts of this book, or otherwise aided the cause: my immediate family; Sherry Berliner, Rabbi Robert and Beile Block, Pamela Coravos, Meyer Freed, Nina Luzzato Gardner, Brendan Gill, Charles Gill, Grace Glueck, Jacques and Aija Graubart, Renee Graubart, Brad Justus, David and Melanie Katzner, Dorothy Kertesz, Rachel Kitzinger, Steven and Nancy Kohn, Emil and Vivian Levin, Andrew Lewin, Daniel Polsby, James Schwartzman, Nancy Seid, Amy Sholiton, Debbie and Bob Stillman, and Leda Zimmerman. Special thanks are in order to Dana Karasik for her speedy and excellent word processing.

Finally, my deepest thanks to two of my friends, Michael Flood, present at the creation, and Valerie Aubry, editor *par excellence*, who pressed me to reach inside myself and write from the heart.

M.G.L.
Marblehead, Massachusetts
September, 1985/
Ellul, 5785

Chapter 1

Goodbye, Fried Clams

Fried clams are not kosher. Did you know that? I used to love fried clams. My fondest memories of high school involve long clam-fry nights at Howard Johnson's, when you could have "All You Can Eat" of the greasy, rubbery delicacies for two dollars and change. The waitresses wore slightly ill expressions when they brought us our fourth and fifth plates. All this is ancient history because five years ago I started to become an Orthodox Jew myself. Goodbye, fried clams.

People who grow up Orthodox do not want to hear about clams. The only thing they are interested in, among all the forbidden foods, is cheeseburgers. I cannot count the number of Orthodox people who have looked at me with an expression that says, "Wow. You've been there. What's it really like?" They all assume that a cheeseburger is the highest form of dining pleasure. Many kinds of cheese, of course, are kosher. Meat, if prepared in keeping with Orthodox ritual, is also kosher. The Bible forbade the combination of meat and milk because it too closely resembled the boiling of a small animal in its mother's milk, a heathen custom apparently prevalent in the time of Moses. Three separate passages in the Bible mention the prohibition of combining meat and milk, and many Jews who do not consider themselves Orthodox still refrain from eating them together.

Cheeseburgers, as we all know, are very good. Bacon cheeseburgers are even better. But my Orthodox friends never asked me about bacon cheeseburgers for the same reason they never asked me about fried clams. Pigs are inherently non-kosher. We will talk about what "kosher" really means, but trust me for now. Pork is irredeemable. Like clams. An observant Jew would never dream of putting either in his or her mouth. So no one even asks about bacon or fried clams. Lobster sometimes. Many observant Jews are interested in lobster, but only from a theoretical standpoint. They know about the bibs and the special equipment for cracking a lobster's claws, and they wonder whether lobsters are as good as people say. Of course, they are that good. So the frequency of questions goes like this: cheeseburgers, always; lobsters, sometimes; but my beloved fried clams, never.

And for me, that is precisely the problem, or at least a metaphor for the problem. Five years ago I began to learn about Orthodox Judaism and started to observe the traditions, including the laws of kosher food. Before that time I had grown up in an assimilated Jewish home in the New York area and had known virtually no Orthodox Jews. My decision to become Orthodox shocked most of my family and friends. I was also greatly surprised. Missionaries from all the various religious cults of the day—the Moonies, the Hare Krishna, Jews for Jesus, the whole lot of them—had approached me in Manhattan over the years. They are unavoidable in New York. But I had never the slightest interest in what they offered. My Jewish religious practice, on the other hand, had been limited to brief, prayerful appearances at the High Holiday services each autumn. I was a happy, stable, fairly average college kid. I did not think of myself as an apt candidate for any movement, let alone for Orthodox Judaism. So what happened?

I am one of those Jews who turned to Orthodoxy. This is my story. I write so that family members and friends of other newcomers to Orthodoxy can understand the process of change, so that Orthodox Jews can better understand their newly observant co-religionists, and so that non-Jews and Jews alike might gain a sense of what being an observant Jew means today. I am not asking you to read this book and become

Orthodox. Rather, I hope that you will read it and understand why others do.

I was never a complete stranger to Judaism. I liked being Jewish. I liked my distant connection with famous Jewish people like the Marx Brothers and Art Shamsky of the '69 Mets. I liked being a part of the People of the Book, even if I never read the Book much. And I liked the symbols: the Torah scrolls, the solemnity of Yom Kippur, the complicatedness of the Passover Seder. My feelings, in short, were similar to those of the bulk of American Jewry. But until five years ago I was content to be little more than a "Jew in my heart," as many people say (one New York rabbi calls this "cardiac Judaism").

Five years ago came my first extended exposure to Orthodox Judaism. I visited an Orthodox yeshiva, or school, in Jerusalem for twelve days, was moved by what I saw, and thought I would try to learn more about Orthodoxy by living as an Orthodox Jew. It was an experiment at first but something clicked. Traditional Judaism and I got along well, despite the sacrifices it entailed: a less active social life, no Mets games Friday nights and Saturday afternoons, and, of course, no more fried clams.

Five years have passed since that first visit to Jerusalem, and until only a few months ago I was still a virtually one hundred percent observant Jew. I wore a yarmulke, or skullcap, in public; I did not eat nonkosher food; I carefully observed the Sabbath laws. I did everything Orthodox Jews do and refrained from everything they refrain from. My purpose: to learn whether it made sense to live in keeping with traditional Jewish law and custom in the modern world, to determine whether Orthodoxy really was the antidote to the ills of modern culture, as some of its backers claimed.

Something was going wrong, though, and it took several years to understand why. When I first considered writing about my experiences with Orthodox Judaism, the book's purpose was to show that a typical assimilated Jew could find his people's traditional way of life so fulfilling that he or she would never turn back. I believed this about myself for a long time. I intended to write a how-to book for baalei teshuva, Jews who become observant. To that end I interviewed many people in Israel and America who had also made the big change, and I sent questionnaires to dozens more who wrote in response to newspaper articles about my research. Most books begin with an acknowledgment of contributors' efforts. This one should begin with an apology to all those who gave of their time to aid the project, because it will be as much about why I am Orthodox no longer as about why I first became religious and what happened along the way. I feel as though I have let down the cause, but I also feel that the cause let me down too.

The problem is this. The most successful baalei teshuva that I met—the Jews who entered Orthodoxy and remained Orthodox ever since—are the ones who most completely cut the ties with their old way of life. Their appearance is different, they live in Orthodox enclaves or in Israel, and they think of themselves primarily as Orthodox and secondarily as Americans, or South Africans, or Democrats, or Mets fans, or anything else.

Although my adherence to ritual was as strict as could be, I never gave up my ties to the nonobservant world. With the exception of a few wonderful people, most Orthodox Jews could not take seriously my commitment to Orthodoxy or think of me as one of their own. Maybe it was just my personality, because many nonobservant Jews have become Orthodox and find the acceptance I so rarely encountered. I think I was a fried clam among Orthodox Jews—something they could not relate to or understand. Now, I had to give up a lot when I became Orthodox. Of all the sacrifices, the hardest was no longer going out with my friends on the weekends. To cut yourself off from your friends and family is to make yourself rather lonely. If the group you have joined—in my case, the Orthodox—cannot fill that void, either because of the way you are or the way they are, you will be quite lonely. No man is an island, even if he is a fried clam. I finally became so lonely and so fed up that I curtailed my strict observance. And here I am today, to tell my story so that the next person interested in Orthodoxy can avoid my mistakes and make a more satisfying adjustment, and so that the Orthodox world can get a better understanding of what fried clams like me are like inside, and so that anyone interested can get an idea of what religious Judaism is all about.

A brief disclaimer: although I am not sure that Orthodox Judaism is right for me, it remains an indisputably wonderful way of life for many people. As will be seen, its emphases on family, on the development of character, and on the importance of community are unquestionably good. In my travels over the last five years in Europe, Israel, the Soviet Union, and America, I met countless models of piety—individuals and families who exemplified the best of what Judaism offers the world. I feel quite ambivalent, frankly, about leaving the fold. There was so much that it does offer, and yet there was so much that I could not stand. If at times I veer between sympathy and frustration, please forgive me. After five years that is how I feel.

Chapter 2

"Tell Him That We Love Him"

On my first visit to Jerusalem, five years ago, I felt myself pulled by an irresistible force, a voice inside that said, "Stay here and learn about a vital part of yourself that you don't understand." I was learning so much in those first days, and I remember wanting to write down exactly what I was feeling, how the moment of metamorphosis felt. Yet I could not. I was assimilating more new information than I could digest. It took a long time to get those initial twelve days into perspective.

How did I get there, and, for that matter, where was I?

A *baal teshuva*, the Hebrew expression for "returnee," is one who has become Orthodox. Since the Six-Day War in 1967, many schools, called "baal teshuva yeshivas," have opened their doors to attract nonreligious young Jewish people, teach them about Jewish history, inculcate in them a reverence for sacred learning, and convince them that they should become Orthodox. One of my closest friends, a college roommate from two years before, had taken his junior year abroad at Hebrew University in Jerusalem. He did not like the secular atmosphere of the university, so he had left it and had entered one of those yeshivas, called Ohr Samayach. I learned this in a telephone conversation with his father. I had called to get Steven's address at Hebrew U. because I was leaving for Europe the next day for a summer study program and intended to spend two weeks in Israel before my studies began.

"Steven's not at Hebrew U. anymore. He's transferred to an Orthodox yeshiva," said Steven's father.

An Orthodox yeshiva? Steven?

"Tell him that we love him and we're behind him in whatever he chooses," said Steven's father. "If he needs money, just tell him to write and ask."

Steven an Orthodox Jew? It made no sense. I knew Steven as a crack tennis player, a writer, and a quiet, thoughtful friend, but I was hard-pressed to think of any connection between him and Judaism. And why Orthodoxy, of all things? I pictured him in a long black coat and a broad-brimmed black hat. You can understand my curiosity and my desire to see what had happened to him. After five or six days in Greece I took a night flight to Tel Aviv and arrived at one in the morning. After a few hours' sleep at the airport I got directions to the yeshiva and took an early bus to Jerusalem. I remember feeling uneasy when I realized that many of the soldiers surrounding me on the bus were younger than I. This was my first contact with Israelis my age. As an American I faced no compulsory military service; as Israelis, they did. Was I feeling a bit guilty? Perhaps.

I found my way to the yeshiva by half past seven. It was already quite warm and humid. Inside the yeshiva I could not find a single person, which seemed odd. I finally found a young Arab boy scrubbing the steps. I asked him whether he knew where Steven Hirsch was, a foolish question since he did not speak English. Instead he motioned me to follow and he took me outside, up a flight of outside stairs and along a stone parapet one floor above ground level. He pointed to an open window and motioned to look inside. I looked in and saw what later turned out to be the main study hall of the yeshiva, the *beit midrash*. The room was packed with silent men bowing, gesticulating, nodding and praying. Many had tallesim—white prayer shawls—pulled over their heads. I had never in my life seen anything like it. The tallesim on the men's heads made the scene resemble a Klan rally. This was Judaism? I was awestruck.

The boy disappeared and I stood watching, rapt, for some time. I had arrived, I learned later, during the *Amidah*, or standing, silent prayer that was the core of the yeshiva's hour-long morning prayer service. I noticed the leather straps and boxes that the men were wearing and assumed that they were tefillin. Starting at the age of thirteen, Orthodox men and boys wear those leather straps and boxes when they pray in the mornings. I was twenty years old and had never seen tefillin before. I had a lot to learn. I kept watching as one man toward the front prayed aloud and the other men punctuated his prayer with "Amen" and other Hebrew words that I could not recognize. This turned out to be the leader's repetition aloud of the *Amidah,* another staple of the morning service.

What happened next surprised me greatly: even though it was not Saturday, the Jewish Sabbath, someone took out a Torah scroll from the ark. (A Torah scroll consists of the first five books of the Bible, Genesis through Deuteronomy, written by hand on special parchment; the ark is a cabinet at the front of a sanctuary where the Torahs are stored.) Was today a Jewish holiday, I wondered. It was not. Part of the prayer service on Monday and Thursday mornings involves a brief reading of the Torah. Mondays and Thursdays, I later learned, were market days in ancient centuries. Jews from the country-side would travel to town on those days and hear the Torah read aloud in order to keep themselves feeling connected. The reading this morning was brief, and the services ended about ten minutes later. Announcements followed and then the room cleared out. Breakfast time. All that praying on an empty stomach. I was impressed.

Impressed? I was bowled over. So this was Orthodoxy. But where was Steven? I wandered into the cafeteria, where eighty or a hundred young men, all wearing skullcaps, were eating and talking. I looked in vain for Steven's face. Maybe he had a long beard now and I did not recognize him. Someone handed me a yarmulke, a skullcap, and asked if he could help. I told him who I was looking for. He asked around and then led me out of the cafeteria.

"He's probably still in his room. Come on."

I followed him outside, up some more stairs and along a

different parapet. Like most buildings in the city, the yeshiva was faced with Jerusalem stone, a yellowish, rough-hewn stone that glistened as it caught the sun's rays and was responsible for the image behind the song "Jerusalem of Gold." The yeshiva and its dormitory was part of an attractive, newly built neighborhood. My guide led me into a dormitory entrance, mounted a flight of stairs, knocked on a door, and left me. I knocked again and tested the handle. The door was unlocked. I entered. There was Steven, sound asleep. When he awoke, he was obviously quite surprised to see me. All I remember of the conversation was Steven asking, "What are you doing here?" and my relief at seeing that he looked the same—no beard, no black hat and coat. What had happened? Why had Steven forsaken big, famous Hebrew U. for a little yeshiva no one had ever heard of?

The Hebrew University of Jerusalem had been designed to satisfy the Steven Hirschs of the world. A dream of the late-nineteenth-century Zionists, the university was to be the place where the Hebrew tradition could take root in its own language and where research in science and medicine would make the desert bloom. The university's history was intimately bound up with that of the modern State of Israel. Albert Einstein gave the first lecture. Scholars exiled from Nazi Germany in the 1930s made Hebrew U. their new home. The institution was living up to the hopes that Chaim Weizmann voiced at the 1918 ceremony honoring the laying of the foundation stone: "In the University the wandering soul of Israel will reach its haven."

If the founders of Hebrew U. had sought to build a university just like any Western university, then from Steven's point of view they had succeeded too well. Campus life was so thoroughly Westernized that Steven felt as though he were back in the States. Many Western visitors to other parts of Israel feel the same disappointment. They want Israel to be a spiritual Disneyland, totally unlike their country of origin, and leave somewhat dejected when they discover that Western culture has made inroads even in the Holy land. In Tel Aviv you can buy pornography in Hebrew as explicit as anything in Times Square and in Netanya you can buy ice cream from a place called "31 Flavors."

The baal teshuva yeshivas employ recruiters who sidle up to Western-looking travelers at the Jerusalem bus station and the Western Wall. The recruiters tell the young men and women that if they have not had a Sabbath meal with a religious family, or if they have not attended a class in a yeshiva, they have not seen the real Israel. While the real Israel also includes the cafe life of Tel Aviv and the most irreligious of the kibbutzim, the collective farms, the recruiters really do have a point. Israel's Jewishness may be hard to deny, but it can be equally hard to perceive. One way to grasp it is to break bread or sit and study with religious Jews.

A friend of Steven's at Hebrew U. was taking classes one night a week at Ohr Samayach, and Steven came along for a session. Steven realized quickly that what he had come to Israel for was here at the little yeshiva and not up the hill at Hebrew University. In mid-semester Steven pulled up his roots at Hebrew U. and moved into the yeshiva. He had been there about three months when I arrived. Steven got dressed—no black hat, no black coat; just khaki pants, and a white shirt. He looked the same as always, much to my relief. He did wear a yarmulke, however, and that was something new.

Curiouser and curiouser. I asked what his morning schedule was like. Steven had already graduated from the beginners' program. As I later learned, the experienced eye could easily tell the beginner's program from a higher-level class. Advanced students were generally paler than the beginners, who looked ruddy and tanned from recent days on the topless beaches of Eilat or the strawberry fields of a kibbutz in the Galilee, or six months in India and Nepal, all places that young Jewish people visit in order to discover something about spirituality. Well, maybe not Eilat. But the kibbutzim and the Great Subcontinent, certainly.

And then the young people come to Jerusalem, and they stand in front of the Western Wall, and they wear the silly cardboard yarmulkes that the guards provide, and stare at the tall remnant of the remaining wall of the Second Temple, sacked by the Romans nineteen hundred years before, and they observe the reverence lavished on the wall by grown men in business suits, old bearded men in caftans, and young soldiers with green uniforms and short, shiny black hair underneath the same cardboard yarmulkes, and those young Western Jews stand there and wonder what it all means to them when suddenly a tall, gaunt figure in black suit and hat has materialized and is speaking to them, suggesting politely that they haven't seen Israel unless they sit in on a class in a yeshiva. And they cannot think of any reason why not, they have time, their flight home does not leave for another four days, and so they come. They arrive open-minded, or suspicious, or just curious. Some stay for an hour, some for a few days, and some never leave.

Steven brought me to the registrar of the yeshiva and explained that I wanted to sit in on a few classes. The registrar took me into his office, which was crammed with enormous, dusty Hebrew books, and asked about my religious background, my education, and my knowledge of Hebrew. He gave me a copy of the beginners' schedule and off I went to class, rubbing my eyes from the brightness of the Jerusalem morning sun, the shock of the new, and a slight feeling of fatigue from my brief slumber on the airport floor. Before me lay a new experience to add to my other experiences. I would be a yeshiva student, if only for a day.

Before the classes came the hard sell. It was nine o'clock. My first class, Talmud, did not begin for half an hour. I wandered back into the beit midrash, the long study hall that had been the scene of all that praying an hour before. The beit midrash did not correspond exactly to a university library, although the back shelves were lined with books. It was too noisy to be a library. As I watched, pairs of young men entered, sat facing each other at the little tables scattered throughout the hall, and opened large, thick texts. They rocked slowly back and forth in their seats and chanted—they would read aloud to each other, then stop to discuss what they had read, and then they would chant some more. I asked two young men seated opposite each other what they were studying and why they studied aloud.

"We're learning *Kiddushin,* which is the volume of the Talmud concerned with the laws of marriage. In yeshiva you learn out loud and with a partner because it forces you to think harder—you have to defend your understanding of the text. You can't get away with sloppy thinking. Where are you from?"

The Talmud. I had only seen the Talmud once before. One morning in Sunday school when I was ten years old they trooped our class into the temple library. This was at a Reform temple in Roslyn, New York. The librarian had us gather around a table and get ready to see something special. He opened up a huge Hebrew volume whose text was printed in ten different typefaces—an L-shaped block of text in the center surrounded by smaller chunks of Hebrew letters. I could read none of it, but I was transfixed before the volume. "The Talmud is the key to knowledge," the librarian was saying, "everything is in here." He told us that the center of the page—the L-shaped block—was the oldest part. The encircling smaller chunks of the text were commentaries on the center block. "This commentary was written by one man," he said, "and this one by his grandson." I remember staring intently at the page, at all those Hebrew letters—wisdom was here, as explained by an ancient scholar and his little grandson. They trooped us out of the library. My talmudic education had begun and ended.

I remember feeling frustrated by wisdom's nearness. But we were taught very little Hebrew at the temple, and I was not about to turn my life upside down and enter a yeshiva where I would learn the Talmud. Not at that point, anyway. And there the matter rested until ten years later, in the beit midrash of Ohr Samayach in Jerusalem, when I found myself looking intently at the same L-shaped block of text.

"Where are you from," the yeshiva student repeated.

"Hmm? From America."

"We're all from America," he said, and his study partner smiled.

"Well, not all. He's from South Africa. Where in the States?"

"From New York. I'm visiting Steven Hirsch."

"Oh, Shlomo," he said, using Steven's Hebrew name, which I had never heard before. "How do you know Shlomo?"

I explained that I had been his roommate at college two years before. "He never mentioned you. Excuse me," he said to the South African, "I'll be back soon. Get started without me."

The South African smiled pleasantly, as if used to interruptions. The other fellow introduced himself to me as Joe and suggested that we take a walk, because it was hard to hold a conversation in the beit midrash. We went outside and walked along a dusty sidewalk. It must have been eighty degrees and it was only ten past nine. Around us were kids straggling to school, mothers pushing baby carriages—the same as America, except that many of the boys wore yarmulkes and the mothers wore kerchiefs around their hair. Joe explained that he had graduated Penn in two years, that he had studied philosophy and had never found any sort of philosophy to live by until he had come to the yeshiva one day. Joe had been visiting the Western Wall when this rabbi, a tall, gaunt figure in a black coat and black hat, asked whether he wanted to visit a yeshiva. That had been eleven months earlier. In that time, Joe continued, he had learned Hebrew, he had learned Aramaic, and now he was learning how to understand the Talmud.

He told me that I was very lucky to have come upon the yeshiva. It was very imporant that I learn about my religion, he said, because life for a Jew is not meaningful without Torah, without study and practice of our ancient traditions. "That's all quite nice," I thought, "but I'm just visiting. It doesn't apply to me directly." We turned back and he brought me to the classroom where the 9:30 Beginning Talmud class was about to start.

Now I was sitting in the classroom, thinking that life was colossally unfair—I had just concluded a difficult semester at college only two weeks before, and here I was awaiting yet another lecture. But this time the teacher was the registrar of the yeshiva, and before him lay a book of the Talmud, open to a tantalizing L-shaped block of text. "He will initiate us," I thought, "he will take us back to the Sunday school library when we were ten years old." And he began.

The subject was the biblical punishment for manslaughter, a cheery topic for a bright June morning. Stoning? Guess again. Hanging? Wrong. Imagine that a person accidentally killed another person—say he was chopping wood in the forest and the axe blade flew off its handle and killed someone. To be fair, the punishment for manslaughter had to be different from the punishment for murder, an intentional crime. One could not let a manslaughterer off scot-free, yet one also had to protect him from harm at the hands of his victim's next of kin. How did the Bible balance these competing needs of punishment and protection, asked the teacher. We looked at each other.

The answer the Bible provides: a form of internal exile based on "cities of refuge," in Hebrew the *aray miklat*. An accidental murderer's punishment was to leave his hometown at once and enter one of those cities of refuge, the founding of which the Bible required once the Jews entered the land of Israel. That seemed remarkable enough.

The Talmud went further, said the teacher. The Talmud wanted to know, what would be the effect of the sudden exile on a person's life? How could the manslaughterer stand the disruption to his family life, to his economic well-being, and to his spiritual existence? All good questions, and the Talmud, said the teacher, had good answers. The Talmud explained that his family would not have to be apart from him. The Levites in charge of the city would set the person up in a trade similar to his trade before the accident—if he was a tanner in Hebron, he'd be a tanner in the city of refuge. If he was a blacksmith in Jericho, he'd be a blacksmith there. But what about his spiritual life, the Talmud asked. And the Talmud answered its own question: since a Jew could not survive without Torah, if the manslaughterer had been a rabbi, then his students would come along. Imagine that, I thought—a prison system so concerned with the wrongdoer's spiritual state that a person would bring his students along if he went into internal exile. The gravity and whimsy of it all touched me.

The teacher continued. How did the system protect the manslaughterer from the victim's family? These were the days of blood feuds, you remember. Again the Talmud had the answer: two *talmidei chachamin*, two wise men versed in the Torah, would accompany the manslaughterer from his hometown to the city of refuge. But not just any two wise men—they had to be big, beefy scholars, the kind whose physiques would dissuade next of kin from carrying on a blood feud. And on the way to the city of refuge, the three could discuss Torah together. How long did the punishment last? Again, said the teacher, the Torah supplied the answer: until the death of the *kohen gadol*, the high priest at the Holy Temple in Jerusalem. For complicated reasons, the death of the high priest signalled a collective amnesty and allowed those in the cities of refuge to return ιc their hometowns.

But wouldn't this lead to a bunch of prisoners wishing death upon the high priest? Perhaps, the Talmud answered. But the solution was simple—the mother of the high priest, and the mothers of all the other priests, would pass their days traveling to each of the cities of refuge to offer solace and cheer to the prisoners. Now how could anyone wish death upon someone who had such a nice mother? Class dismissed.

It was not what I had anticipated. What did I expect of a Talmud class? Kabbalistic secrets passed on in hushed tones or clues to the meaning of life—but not a prison system featuring the high priest's mother as Florence Nightingale. It was too light-hearted to be religious. Religion was supposed to be somber and incomprehensible. I had to know more.

Fortunately, the next class was one in a series concerned with how all the pieces of the puzzle fit together—the prayers, the yarmulkes, the Bible, and everything else. Just what I needed. Now, the building had no air-conditioning. It was ten-thirty and even inside it was terribly hot and sticky. How could people concentrate on their studies, I wondered. On the way to the next classroom we walked along the parapet overlooking the beit midrash and passed the window through which I had viewed the praying that morning. I looked in and saw that the room was packed with pairs of animated young men sitting opposite each other and chanting or arguing or thinking. No one seemed to mind the noise. The scene resembled a chorus rehearsal with each vocalist singing from a different score.

And on into the next classroom. Structures of Orthodox Judaism. The topic this morning was Jewish law—where it came from and why people studied it. The rabbi spoke essentially as follows:

"Suspend your disbelief," he told us. "Don't look at the material as you would in a university. Try to view the material as the Jewish people always did—with belief as a starting point and not as a goal. I'm not asking you to change inside. I'm not asking you to be a different person from the way you are. But I do want you to play ball with me, so that you can understand where Orthodoxy is coming from."

Then came the first dose of theology in the three hours since my arrival.

"We believe—traditional Judaism has always believed—that the source of law and morality in the world is God, and that God spoke to certain people who were, let us say, attuned to God's message. They were more capable than others in their generation of hearing God speak. Abraham was such a man. Isaac and Jacob were such men. Joseph, the interpreter of dreams, was such a man. But above all was Moses. Moses, the Jewish people have traditionally believed, was the one man who spoke to God face to face, who twice spent forty days and forty nights on the top of Mount Sinai without food, without drink, without sleep, drinking in only the law—learning what God wanted from every person. When Moses came along God said this is the person I can turn to. And God turned to Moses and He explained everything to him. How the world was created. The history of the world up until that point. That God wanted to bring the Jewish people close to him, and that the way to attain this closeness to God was to follow the laws that God dictated to Moses.

"Moses was a teacher. We call him in Hebrew, *Moshe Rabbeinu*, 'Moses, our teacher.' When he came down from the mountain he taught it all to the Jews. This was just after the Exodus from Egypt. The children of Israel were living in the desert, apart from the contaminations of civilization, preparing themselves, cleansing themselves, readying themselves. To do what? What was the focus of the preparation?

"Learning. Learning and practicing. Learning and practicing and drawing closer to God. Learning the laws that God had taught Moses. Practicing what those laws demanded—a higher level of morality than the world had ever known. And through study and practice of God's laws came the ultimate reward— getting to know God, getting to understand God's purpose for the world.

"The Torah—the compilation of God's words and God's laws—is compared in our tradition to a blueprint. God created the world by looking at the blueprint and acting. A builder needs a blueprint to build a house, and God, as it were, needed a blueprint in order to create the universe. And the Torah is that blueprint. And the Jewish people has always seen its highest purpose as sitting down and learning—learning that blueprint, learning what God had in mind, learning what our purpose is, learning why we were brought into existence, learning why we are here.

"And where is this Torah? As it says in *Dvarim*—the Book of Deuteronomy—'It is not in heaven, so that you might say, "Oh, who shall go up for us to heaven, and bring it to us?" Nor is it across the sea, that one should say, "Oh, who will cross the sea for us and bring it to us?" Because the word is very close to you, it is in your mouth and in your heart!' 'Your mouth and your heart.' When you see the *bochrim*—the yeshiva students— poring over their texts, they are doing exactly what I'm talking about. They are studying that blueprint, learning to understand, learning so that they can practice and live by God's laws, learning so that they can pass on to their children and their children's children what Yiddishkeit is, what Judaism is, what Torah is. And that is what this yeshiva is for. To give people whose backgrounds did not include Torah a chance to learn Torah, to learn for themselves what it means to live as a Jew.

"Think about yourselves for a moment. Your immediate families may not have been observant. But your grandparents might have been. Your great-grandparents almost certainly were. And so were their parents, and theirs, and theirs— despite poverty, despite pogroms, despite bigotry, for all those centuries your families kept to their faith. The ancient Romans could not stamp out Judaism, as hard as they tried. They destroyed the Holy Temple in Jerusalem and colonized the land of Israel but they could not crush Judaism. The Nazis could not stamp out Judaism, as hard as they tried. They could wipe out the Jewish population of entire towns, put to death six million of our people, but they could not erase Yiddishkeit.

"How could this people have survived all the powerful nations bent on destroying them if it weren't for some spark of Godliness behind them, something not of this world? But I'm not asking you to believe that, or to believe anything I have told you—about Moses, about blueprints, about anything. The important thing is to remember that the key to understanding Judaism is to understand the texts and the laws, the letter and the spirit. And if you want to understand what it means to be Jewish, what Jewish history is, what your place in Judaism is, you have to put some time into learning it. And the purpose of this yeshiva is to make a place for you so that you can learn, and then once you understand it, you can make up your own mind about do I believe this, does that make any sense. And you can come to a decision for yourselves about what the best way is for a person to live. Any questions?"

Many questions. The rabbi fielded them deftly. The class asked about non-Jews and how they fit into the picture— whether it was right that God should play favorites among the peoples of the world. They asked how evil could exist in a world created by a perfect God; why fixed, communal prayer played such an important role in Judaism instead of heartfelt prayers as devised by individuals reflecting upon their own needs and concerns. They asked how the biblical account of creation could be reconciled with evolution, and whether it made sense to keep to ancient dietary laws when advances in food preparation had obviated the concerns that led to those dietary laws in the first place (for example, why can't we eat our old irredeemable friend, the pig). I asked why Orthodoxy distinguished between men and women in the realm of ritual.

In short, a roomful of young people were coming face to face with an aspect of themselves they had never understood before. In the rabbi they had a forceful speaker with an organized mind who might provide answers to questions that had been hovering close to the surface or had been lurking in the subconscious. We all seemed to feel the pleasure of release when we asked our questions—we had a chance to voice our frustration over being Jewish and not knowing what being Jewish meant. The act of asking had transformed us, if ever so slightly.

The answers themselves were frustrating. The rabbi did speak well. He tried to give a nutshell version of Orthodoxy's responses to the questions, but the answers were too pat. Things were clearly more complex than he could explain with a few sentences. To be fair, one could see frustration flicker across the rabbi's face as he attempted to give satisfying answers, knowing as he must have that each question was one that had perplexed the great thinkers for generations, that brief answers could never be satisfying, that each answer only raised more hard questions, and that each young man in the room had, in effect, placed Judaism on trial. The rabbi might have sensed himself a defense attorney for the faith, aware that if his audience did not like his answers they could walk out of the yeshiva, leave Israel, and never give their relation to their religion a second thought. I admired the rabbi for what he was trying to do, and I saw myself one day doing the same thing—

preaching to the unconverted masses, refuting arguments in dazzling fashion, bringing souls back to the fold. Then I remembered that I was one of the unconverted masses myself.

The class ended and it was time for afternoon prayers. The beit midrash filled again with young men for a brief fifteen-minute service. As if all the praying they had done that morning wasn't good enough. Someone handed me a bilingual prayer book and pointed out the pages, but I preferred to watch the rest of them. How many times a day did one pray here, I wondered. Surely not five times, like the Moslems, I hoped.

Lunchtime. Joe and Steven decided to forego the yeshiva cafeteria's offering ("we'll see it again at dinner," they said) and we walked to a falafel stand down the street. They asked me how I liked yeshiva so far.

"I never expected the Talmud to have a sense of humor about manslaughter," I said.

"The Talmud has a sense of humor about a lot of things," said Joe. I asked them whether the yeshiva would mind if I slept there for a couple of nights. After the weekend—today was Thursday—I intended to track down two college friends who were in Israel working on a kibbutz.

When I think now about those last two points—whether the yeshiva would mind and whether I could trace my friends—I have to smile at my colossal naivete. The yeshiva wanted me to stay, was hoping that I would stay, was prepared to go to great lengths to make me want to stay. Their thinking was clear—if I would come for the morning, I might not leave until after the Jewish Sabbath Friday night and Saturday; if I stayed for the Sabbath I might put in a week; and so on until a year passed and I came to the decision that living the life of a Torah Jew, whatever that meant, was the right thing. I had no such intentions, of course.

My adviser in the ancient Greek department at my college had helped secure for me a place in a small summer program in Greece that offered the courses I needed to finish a Greek major. I had given the program directors my word that I would attend, and there was no chance of my reneging. Over falafel Joe asked me what was so important about ancient Greek, which nobody speaks, compared with Hebrew and Aramaic, which would allow me to converse with the greatest minds of our people. This mild burst of anti-intellectualism from a philosophy major surprised me. I told him so. He smiled and said that I would have to meet a friend of theirs, Adin, who as Danny had given up studying Classics at Cambridge to come to Ohr Samayach. I would meet Adin, I said, but I was going to Greece.

Now, about the friends on kibbutz. I do not know where I got the idea, but I believed that somewhere in Tel Aviv, the commercial center of Israel, there existed a "Kibbutz Desk" which had up-to-the-minute rosters of foreigners working at every kibbutz in the country. All one needed to do was find this desk, give the polite attendant one's friends' names, get the location of the kibbutz, and off one would go. If you have ever been to Israel, you know that things do not work quite so smoothly. There is no such Kibbutz Desk. Some of the kibbutzim may not even know what foreigners are working there. Even if they did, they probably could not be bothered to send a list of anything to anyone. If you come from New York and you have dealings with any level of Israeli bureaucracy, watch your blood pressure. It will soar. But at the time I knew nothing of this. To my mind, a country that could make the desert bloom could surely locate two American backpackers within its borders. Anyway, back to lunch.

"How often does the yeshiva pray together?" I asked.

"Three times a day—a long service in the morning and two shorter ones, in the afternoon and in the evenings," Steven answered.

"Why so often?"

"Long story."

"Do all Orthodox Jews pray three times a day?"

"They're supposed to."

"Even Orthodox Jews not in yeshiva?"

"Everybody."

They ate only kosher food, they studied ancient texts, and they prayed three times every day. Orthodoxy was turning out to be far different from the idea of Judaism I had grown up with, mainly involving cameo appearances at the High Holiday services and the Seder table. This was turning into a high-demand religion. I wondered how Steven could stand it. I wondered how anyone could stand it. At that moment there was no danger of my becoming Orthodox. The sense of picking up where I had left off in the Sunday school library ten years before was quite exciting, and I was curious about the Sabbath. But come Sunday I was bound for Tel Aviv and my imaginary Kibbutz Desk. We finished our falafels and bought some cookies—a truly balanced meal. The noonday sun broiled the street as we returned to the yeshiva. Nap time.

Chapter 3

A Spy in the House of God

All I wanted to do was sleep. Back in the dormitory I stripped down to my shorts and unrolled my sleeping bag. But the heat and humidity made sleep impossible. I tossed about and tried to make sense of all I had seen that morning. I remembered hearing a lecture the year before on missionary cults and their attractiveness to Jewish young people. A day in the life of a Hare Krishna recruit, I learned, begins early in the morning with group chanting, and, oddly enough, McDonald's quarter-pounders—a cheap source of protein. Thus fortified, the recruit spends a long day cadging change on an assigned street corner. Americans are so generous that the average daily take for each such recruit is one hundred or one hundred twenty-five dollars. Multiply that hundred dollars by the number of days in the year, and multiply that figure by the thousands upon thousands of young people caught up in the cults, and the annual income of the groups is astounding. Their only big expenditures are for housing and quarter-pounders.

A high proportion of these recruits are Jewish kids, the lecturer said. Interestingly, he laid the blame for the cult phenomenon at the doorstep of American Jewish institutions that do such a poor job educating Jewish young people about their own faith.

If the Judaism they grow up with seems sterile and devoid of spirituality, young people will naturally turn elsewhere. Parents of Jewish kids who join cults generally think they have done the right thing by limiting their children's exposure to

Judaism. To the parents, Judaism means guilt and backwardness, poverty and the Holocaust. But even the kids who have some Jewish education, said the speaker, possess such a poor impression of their religion that they believe that their need for a spiritual dimension can only be satisfied outside the faith. And the cults swoop down and grab these well-intentioned young people by the busload.

I wondered whether the lecturer, a New York area rabbi, knew about Ohr Samayach and similar institutions here in Jerusalem. I was sure that he would be delighted by them, since they did exactly what he thought American Jewish institutions were failing at—namely, presenting Judaism in the best possible light and offering Jewish young people like me a chance to ask questions, learn the texts, and make up our own minds. When I returned to America three months later the irony of these thoughts was not lost on me. Many of my friends and family thought that Ohr Samayach's brand of Orthodoxy was itself a cult, and that I had been brainwashed. But I had heard that lecture and I knew that the cults were all non-Jewish groups. Orthodox Judaism was the antithesis of cults, I thought. How misguided my family and friends were, I thought.

At that moment, however, I was not so sure. In my first few hours at the yeshiva I had encountered several bursts of hard sell ("Why go to Greece? Your people needs you here!") and had listened to the rolling cadences and powerful arguments of the rabbi in the second class. I was fascinated by what I was learning, but I was a bit put off by the need of virtually everyone I met to convince me to stay. Sleep overcame me at last. When I awoke, several hours later, I realized that I had slept through the next class on my schedule. Just as well—I needed a break before my emotions were wrung out all over again. A knock on the door—it was Joe to collect me for a 4:30 Bible class. I rubbed my eyes and off we went.

On the way to the lecture Joe asked me if I knew about the idea of weekly portions of the Torah. I did, and I felt proud to know something after this long day's introduction to my ignorance about Judaism. The written Torah—the Five Books of Moses, Genesis through Deuteronomy—was long ago divided into fifty-four weekly portions. If you were Bar or Bat Mitzvah you knew this because you lived with your assigned portion for months of preparation and anxiety before the big day. Many Jewish people who know little and care less about religion still have a warm place in their heart for "their" portion. Mine came from Deuteronomy; I chanted it as a thirteen-year-old and understood it only slightly at the time. Joe explained that the portion this week was *Shlach* (beginning at Numbers 13:1). *Shlach* recounts the episode of the spies. Did I know about the spies? No, I said, reverting to (ignorant) form. Joe explained that while many of the boys had been studying the weekly portion, or *parasha*, by themselves, every Thursday afternoon one of the rabbis would give a class in it for students of all levels of attainment. It was to that lecture that we headed.

The room was jammed with newcomers in their T-shirts and jeans and old-timers in dark slacks and white button-down shirts. We found two places on a side bench. *Chumashim*— Hebrew Bibles—appeared from nowhere. Students shared, two or three boys to a book. The rabbi came in carrying a Hebrew text—it turned out to be a large, commentary-filled copy of the Book of Numbers—and the entire class rocketed to its feet. "Why did we do that," I whispered. "Respect," Joe whispered back. That was new to me—a class rising to its feet to honor its teacher. The rabbi sat down, and the class followed suit. Now, to me, growing up, Bible stories were simply stories. Then, during my freshman year at Amherst, I took a class in Jewish Scripture and learned that the Bible could be taken seriously as literature. At that time, of course, I did not know how seriously it could be taken.

The class began now, the rabbi first reading selectively in Hebrew and then translating roughly into English: "And the Lord spoke to Moses saying, 'Send yourself men to spy out the land of Canaan, which I am giving to the children of Israel.' . . . And Moses sent them to spy out the land of Canaan, and said to them, 'Go up this way southward, and go up into the hill country, and see the land and how it is, and the people that live in it, whether they are strong or weak, few or many, and what the cities that they live in are like, whether they are tent cities or fortresses, and what the land is, whether it be fat or lean. And be strong—have courage."

The rabbi spoke clearly and intelligently about his topic—how Jewish scholars interpreted the story of the spies, and what light the story shed on the relationship of the Jewish people to their God while they were still living in the desert. In the five years since that Thursday afternoon, the story of the spies has become "my" portion even more than the portion I read at my Bar Mitzvah. In the yeshiva I felt like a spy myself. I was a foreigner surveying the land and the religion of Israel. I had gone southward into the hill country of Jerusalem and I was seeing the land, and how it was, and the people who lived and practiced its ancient religion, and I was trying to be strong and have courage as I faced this unknown part of myself. A spy in the house of God.

A biblical text has many levels, the rabbi explained, begging the indulgence of the students who knew this already. The level of *pshat* is the surface level of ordinary meaning. *Remez* is the next, slightly deeper level. *Remez* is Hebrew for "hint." On this second level, things are not stated directly—the text provides the astute reader with nothing more than clues to its deeper meaning. *Drosh* comes next. *Drosh* has to do with the elucidation of the ideas that the two simpler levels may suggest. Finally comes *sod*, Hebrew for "foundation" or "base" and also for "secret." At its base, every line, every word, every letter, every curlicue on every letter in the Bible has a *sod* meaning intelligible to only a few people in each generation, according to tradition. *PaRDeS*, an acronym composed of the initial letters of the names of the four levels of biblical study, *pshat*, *remez*, *drosh*, and *sod*, is also the Hebrew word for "grove" or "orchard." This symbolizes, the rabbi explained, that studying the Bible is like entering a fragrant grove—it offers pleasure on many levels.

A cardinal principle of biblical study, he continued, is that every word or letter in the Bible is there for a reason. If a letter or word seems extraneous it is the reader's job to determine what it is doing there. Take the first sentence in our text. "And the Lord spoke to Moses, saying, 'Send yourself men, to spy out the land of Canaan, which I am giving to the children of Israel.' " By this time Moses had led the Jews on the Exodus from Egypt, and the Jews had stood before a trembling Mount Sinai, had heard God's voice, and had been given the Ten Commandments. Despite all they had been through, however, the Jews did not trust God to keep them alive and bring them into the Promised Land. The Jews were a slave people turned into an army overnight, and sudden conversions do not always last, the rabbi said rather pointedly. This business about the spies reflected the lack of faith of the Jews in their exasperated God.

Other classical commentators read other things into the verse, said the rabbi, but this reading was the generally accepted one, the interpretation that has enjoyed a centuries-old imprimatur among Jewish scholars. He lifted up his copy of Numbers and pointed out a rectangle of Hebrew text. He explained that this rectangle contained about five verses from the Bible. On the rest of the page, and the facing page, in varying sizes of Hebrew print, were commentaries by eight or ten leading scholars dating back hundreds of years, arranged in a tidy, hypnotic symmetry. Have you ever seen a Hebrew text of one book of the Bible, swarming with Hebrew writing, the thin and thick lines and curves jostling with each other and competing for your attention? I had never known how seriously the Torah was taken, how many man-centuries of disinterested piety and scholarship had gone into the edition that the teacher was holding before us. He held the book open and pointed.

"This is Rashi, whose commentary is preserved in a sort of italicized Hebrew. This is Ibn Ezra, in this corner. He lived in Spain in the twelfth century. These columns are by the Ramban, as Nachmanides was called. He lived in Spain at the same time. This small section is Sforno's contribution. He came from Italy and wrote in the sixteenth century." He turned the page to show us that each of the commentators continued in just the same place on the page relative to the other authors. A few of the boys in white shirts shifted uncomfortably on their benches. They knew all this and were waiting impatiently for the rabbi to end the show-and-tell phase of class and pierce the deeper meaning of the week's portion. But I was hooked.

At Amherst, I was a language student majoring in English and ancient Greek with a sort of minor in French. That semester I had read Plato, Chaucer, and Proust, each in his original language. Proust was partly Jewish, and reading him I was fascinated by the hints at his complicated relation to his religion. Proust operating on the level of *remez*, I thought now. But those pages of squared-off scholarship in Hebrew—the secret language whose writing I could pronounce but not understand—those pages of elegant Hebrew letters excited me more than I can describe. True, they lacked the solemn mystery of the Talmud's great L-shaped blocks of text, but that symmetry, those letters all demanding to be read and understood—the fruits of the scholarship of my people! I had to know what those letters said.

I did not know what the Torah contained, aside from general things like the Ten Commandments and the creation of the world. But clearly, here was scholarship, here was literature untainted by the anti-Semitism of the French upper classes that Proust wrote about in connection with the Dreyfus affair, unmarred by Chaucer's ribald portrayals of Jews as devils. In those two pages I saw Jews reaching the limits of their potential in the role that they had been assigned by God, or had assigned themselves—interpreters of God's word, grasping the hidden meanings of seemingly extraneous letters and distilling from those meanings—why, the blueprint! Grasping the blueprint by which God the Architect had constructed the world! Grasping the purpose and meaning of life!

I sat on that wobbly bench, its paint cracked and peeling, body to body with six other young men, the sweat pouring down my shirt from the heat and the closeness of other bodies in the room packed with bodies, bodies rocking slowly, young men fingering their beards, listening with care to every word the rabbi spoke, or looking intensely bored—one sat methodically picking his nose for most of the hour. I sat on that wobbly bench and I thought, "I have to learn this. I have to learn the language and the history and the texts and the commentaries. I have to learn everything. I have to be a rabbi, if that is what it takes to understand it all. I have to know."

It was not until much later that I learned how the story of the spies came out. Moses appointed one prince from each tribe—an early form of blue-ribbon commission—and they entered Canaan, made their rounds, and made their report. Ten of the princes lied. They spread rumors throughout the Jews' desert camp that Canaan was barren, inhospitable, and filled with unconquerable giants. The frightened people sought to depose Moses and elect a new leader to bring them back to Egypt. True slave mentality. God, furious, told Moses that He would destroy the entire people on the spot, but for Moses and the two princes who told the truth about the land's greatness.

In the end, God relented: although the adults responsible for the mutiny would die in the desert as old age overtook them, their children and grandchildren would be given the land of Israel. "Them will I bring in," God told Moses, "and they shall know the land which ye have despised." As powerful as the story is, representing God as a long-suffering deity filled with patience until overwhelmed by provocation, its denouement seemed flat compared with the fever pitch into which I was thrust by my discovery of all that commentary. The spy in the house of God had a lot to report.

Chapter 4

"Like, How Many Children Do You Want to Have?"

I needed to find someone, anyone, to tell about everything I had seen and learned in this never-ending day. The beginners' schedule called for one more class that evening, but I could not absorb another drop of new material. The day had begun with my peep through the parapet window onto the praying men early that morning and continued with introductions to Talmud, biblical criticism, and hard sell ("Why go to Greece? Your people needs you here"). I had worn myself out with learning. Steven had an engagement that evening that he could not break, so he would not have to bear my babbling about what he had known for months. At that moment I found myself admiring his courage for joining the yeshiva and learning full-time, and for the first moment since my arrival I wanted to do the same.

"Did you just come in today?"

It was one of the other students in the beginners' program. He introduced himself as Frank and suggested that we go to the center of town and have a beer. "I hope he's a good listener," I thought, and off we went. Our bus climbed through Mea Shearim, which Frank told me was a century-old neighborhood filled with religious Jews. The streets were packed with people wheeling shopping carts and baby carriages. One heavily bearded man in a long black coat—just as I had pictured Steven—was pushing a baby carriage filled with eggs.

"Getting ready for Shabbos," Frank explained.

Frank was a tall, handsome, bearded fellow who had been at Ohr Samayach for four weeks but whose skin was still dark from three months of grape-picking in Southern France. He had learned of Ohr Samayach from other young people at the vineyard and wanted to see Israel and the yeshiva before he went back to the States and graduate school. We went to a bar he knew on Jaffa Street, the main street of downtown Jerusalem, not far from the walls of the Old City. Frank said that he came there frequently in the evenings "just to keep a little balance in my life." I could see his point. Although I had been in yeshiva only one day I felt relieved to see people sitting and drinking, comfortable in jeans and T-shirts, oblivious to the search for truth and meaning going on in yeshivas all over Jerusalem. It was also a relief to see women again. The only women I had seen that day were the kerchiefed mothers pushing strollers early that morning. I wanted to ask Frank why the yeshiva was all-male and what women did if they wanted to study.

The bar was in an alley between two buildings. People sat at small tables underneath trees whose branches were lit by small white lights. The alley's stone walls must never have been exposed to direct sunlight, for the stones were cool and almost moist to the touch. We chose a table and Frank ordered two Maccabee beers, the beer of Israel named for the priestly family that led the revolt against the Greeks remembered at Hanukah. You remember Judah Maccabee.

"That's the funny thing about Israel," Frank said. "It never lets you forget for a moment where you are. Even the beer makes you think of Bible class."

(Several years later I would remember that moment as I had another apt reminder of how Israel constantly and unconsciously reminds itself that it is Israel. I was watching "Kojak" on Israeli television one night in 1982. The program was broadcast in English and subtitled in Hebrew and Arabic. I used to work on my conversational Hebrew by comparing the dialogue with the subtitles on the screen. Someone rushed in to give Kojak some news, but the bald-headed detective snarled, "What does that have to do with the price of tea in China?" The subtitle gave the Hebrew idiomatic equivalent—"What does Mount Sinai have to do with the Sabbatical year?"—a phrase I recognized as a question posed by Rashi, an eleventh century biblical and talmudic scholar, in his commentary on the Book of Leviticus.* In Israel, even Kojak talks Torah.)

The waitress returned with the beers, and Frank asked me how I liked the yeshiva. I remember unleashing a torrent of words, unburdening myself of all I had seen since my arrival. Frank was patient and heard me out.

"I felt the same way when I got here," he said. "A lot of people do. It's very exciting."

I looked around the bar and felt rather conspiratorial, as if only Frank and I were in on the Big Secret. I asked him if he intended to remain long at the yeshiva. His answer surprised me.

"Only a week more. The rabbis are giving me a hard time. They tell me I'm wrong when I say that I can take what I've learned here in a month and go out into the world and survive. They even get after me in class—'Frank thinks a month is long enough to learn the entire Torah!'

"But I have a grip on the basics, on why we believe various things, and why we do various things, and I think I'll be O.K."

A month did not sound like a long time. I had heard more than once today that the best way to gain competence in Orthodox practice, including Talmud study, was to put in no less than two full years. Joe had said as much at lunch—that life was like a number line stretching from one to seventy or eighty, and giving up one or two years out of a lifetime was a small sacrifice compared to the gain that a person, his family, and his people would reap.

"Oh, I've heard that bit about the number line myself." Frank said evenly. "But I just don't think I need two years. I

---

*The Bible commands farmers in the land of Israel to let their land lie fallow during every seventh, or Sabbatical, year. The commandment appears directly before a reference to Mount Sinai, a juxtaposition that biblical scholars felt compelled to explain.

think I have what I need." As impressed as I was that Steven wanted to stay on indefinitely, I was equally impressed at Frank's capacity to resist.

"Don't get me wrong. I don't take lightly what they do here. The teachers are really good, and they challenge your thinking and they challenge the way you look at the world. I'm also into the idea of learning Judaism from the original texts, instead of learning about Judaism from someone else's interpretations. But I just don't think I want to stay much longer."

I wanted to ask how a person who had just been exposed to the yeshiva could walk away so calmly, but I did not think it polite. Instead I asked him about women—why there were none at the yeshiva.

"There's a women's branch of the yeshiva across town. Most guys don't even know where it is. They study the same stuff we do, with more of an emphasis on Bible and less of an emphasis on Talmud.* Basically, Orthodox Judaism doesn't believe that it's legitimate for men and women to sit and study Torah together. I once asked a rabbi why, and he told me that studying Torah has to be done in pairs, the way you see it in the beit midrash. You really get into the thinking of the other person. It's day after day, hour after hour. You know the other person's mind backwards and forwards. You're closer with your *chavruta*—your study partner—than some married couples are. So the rabbis said that guys and girls don't learn together because the momentum from all that closeness can just pick you up and carry you into bed. It's sort of a far-out explanation."

"Do you believe it," I asked.

Frank smiled.

"Sort of."

He asked me whether I knew anything about the social situation in the yeshiva world. I shook my head, and he

---

*Traditionally, only men and boys studied Talmud because the rabbis believed that womens' minds were not suited for the intense intellectual exercise required. This attitude has been changing of late. Many Orthodox young women now learn Talmud. Most yeshivas for newcomers offer women and men the same curriculum.

proceeded to outline for me what I later learned was essentially the truth.

"It's very different from the non-*frum* world," he began, using the Yiddish term for "Orthodox." "First of all, there's no random dating. You just don't call someone up and say, 'Let's go to a movie,' and you never come to a place like this bar to meet women. You learn in yeshiva for a while—six months, a year, whatever—and then, when you're ready to get married, you tell the rabbis. The rabbis and some of their wives also teach in the girls' school. So by the time you're ready to get married, they have a good idea of who is available and who would be well-suited for you.

"They talk to the girl," Frank continued. "By now she is in the same position you are—she's been in yeshiva for the last year or so, and she wants to find a guy and get married—and if you sound O.K. to her, you meet for coffee or you go to a hotel lobby and you just sit and talk. You get to know each other. No mind-games, no questions like 'Is he being nice to me because he wants to get into my pants?' You just ask each other questions."

"Like what?"

"Like, how many children do you want to have, where do you want to live—America or Israel. What level are you on in Orthodoxy? I mean, there are levels—some people do one thing, and other people say you don't have to do that. You have to make sure you mesh. It's hard to believe, but they ask each other these things on the first or second date.

"The key is finding the right place to go. There are rules. You can't go just anywhere. You have to find a place that's public enough so it doesn't look like you've got something illicit in mind, and quiet enough so that you can do all this serious talking. Most people like hotel lobbies—they're pretty safe."

What made a hotel lobby safe? What was to keep the couple from checking in to a room, especially if they were learning how much they had in common?

"If you like her, you don't call her back," Frank continued. "You check it out with the *shadchan*, the person who set the two of you up together. That way, if she didn't like you, it spares her from having to reject you in person or over the phone, and it saves you from getting shot down. It's pretty clever—nobody gets hurt. If you did like her, and if she did like you, then you both find out from the shadchan—the go-between—and you call her up, and then you go out again. Same deal. No kiss goodnight, and you certainly don't go to bed with her. That just doesn't happen. I mean it does happen—you hear about 'tefillin dates,' where a frum guy sleeps with some chick and brings his tefillin so that he can pray in the morning. But that's mostly with guys who are just getting into Orthodoxy. After a while you sort of have to make up your mind. Either you're in it or you're not.

"So there you are on the second date. Now, if you liked each other, things start to happen really fast. Your head can spin. Word travels fast in a yeshiva that you've gone out with the same girl twice in a row, and everybody starts asking if you're serious about her. Serious! I've gone out with the same girl twice before I even knew her last name!

"And she's getting the same treatment at the girls' yeshiva. You see her a couple more times—now you do something really daring on a date—you don't go to a hotel lobby, you go to the Biblical Zoo, or you buy her a big dinner at some restaurant. And then everyone is asking you when you're going to propose.

"And either you propose—you've only known her about two months, but by then you know everything about her—her family, her education, her attitude toward religion, everything—or the two of you break it off. If you don't break it off, and you get married, then there's an incredibly big yeshiva wedding.

"Everybody comes—all the guys, all the girls from the girls' school, all the rabbis. And everybody dances and drinks and eats and checks each other out, and by the end of the evening the yeshiva has another married couple and the rabbis are getting a bunch of inquiries from the guys and the girls—is that one available? Would this one be interested in me even though

I wasn't born Orthodox? And the whole thing starts all over again."

My head was spinning. We ordered two more Maccabees and I asked Frank if he had ever been on one of those set-up dates, and again I was surprised by his answer.

"No. I've only been here a month. That's not long enough for these rabbis to take you seriously. You have to be here a while before they know how committed you are to Torah, and who would be good for you."

He paused. "I'm not sure that I'd like to meet someone that way. But I do think the system has advantages over the way we do things in the outside world. The part about being careful not to hurt the other person, the part about no casual sex—that isn't so bad because that's where people get hurt all the time. And it makes life a lot easier than having to call up some girl out of the blue. The rabbis have sort of approved you, and the guys say that that makes the first date much easier. But, to be honest, I haven't had much trouble getting girls, and I would sort of miss the spontaneity, you know, the thrill of the chase.

"The thing is, though, even though it sounds crazy, not calling the girl back until you get an O.K. from a rabbi, and the whole bit—the thing is, it's part of the system, and the system works. These marriages stay together more than marriages do in the non-frum world. The couples are closer. One of the guys even told me that the sex was better with his wife that he met on a blind date than with the chicks he used to meet in bars. It's just better if you didn't meet your future husband or wife at a bar or a disco or some pick-up scene. It's better this way, not to have your marriage founded on, you know, founded on b.s."

"Then why are you leaving," I asked.

"I don't know. B.S. can be fun. Maybe I'm just not ready for this."

I was accustomed to making friends with women through college classes and activities and not in singles bars, but nonetheless, Frank's description of the aimlessness of secular social life struck a chord. We paid and left, walking home through the nighttime streets of Mea Shearim, the religious neighborhood.

Neither of us spoke for some time. We took an unlit, winding path off one of the main streets. We could smell bread baking. It was past eleven o'clock. Frank explained that many Jerusalem bakeries stayed open all night Thursday preparing challah rolls—twisted loaves—for the Sabbath tables of Friday night and Saturday afternoon. At the end of the path was one such bakery, teeming inside with bearded young men wearing black *kippot* (skullcaps) pinned to their hair, preparing rack upon rack of newly baked challah while flour dust flew in the air and settled over everything.

We stood and watched the silent commotion, the young men baking noiselessly so as not to disturb the sleep of the neighborhood. Frank spoke to one of the bakers and a little money changed hands. The baker handed us each a steaming-hot challah. I tore mine open and bit into the heat and the bread. As we ate, we watched the young men shove more racks of dough into the large ovens. We finished our challot and walked through the tiny, winding streets back to the yeshiva. We said goodnight and I found my way back to my sleeping bag. I stripped down and climbed in. Only moments passed before I drifted off. "And there was morning, and there was evening," I thought, "one day."

Chapter 5

Angel's Advocate

When I woke up the next morning, Friday morning, I intended to spend a few more days in the yeshiva and then wander into Tel Aviv to look for my imaginary Kibbutz Desk. I would find my friends' kibbutz, get a taste of that aspect of Israeli life, and then take my charter flight to Greece on the nineteenth. Two days later, I would board an overnight boat to Crete, where I would meet the group with whom I was to spend the summer. Two plays in ancient Greek—Sophocles' *Oedipus the King* and Aristophanes' comedy *The Birds*—were to be my summer reading. And then back to America for senior year.

Twelve days later, my plans had changed. I had long since given up on the Kibbutz Desk and the idea of finding my friends—someone must have disabused me of that aspect of my naivete. I still intended to go to Greece, having given my word that I would attend the program. But I had decided to return to the yeshiva at summer's end, enroll full-time, live there, spend a year or two learning Talmud, Bible, and practical Jewish law and customs, and then come back to America and finish college. I would trade, at least temporarily, the Amherst campus for the world of the beit midrash.

No one locked me in a motel room and deprived me of sleep and food until I promised to come back to the yeshiva. No one strapped me to a device that shot electric current through my brain; no one woke me at five in the morning, fed me quarter-pounders, made me sit through two hours of chanting, and then sent me into the street to beg change from strangers. My family and friends will never believe this, but I made the decision by myself to return to yeshiva—I was not coerced. During those twelve days at the yeshiva I often wondered whether what I was experiencing had parallels to cult indoctrination; whether I was actually being "brainwashed." I silenced those fears by thinking that since there was no physical force, there could be no brainwashing.

There were no locked gates—one could walk or take a bus to the center of Jerusalem and leave the yeshiva behind, something Frank would do that week. There were no threats like "if you leave here you know your life will be ruined," although rabbis and students did cajole the waverers ("Why go to Greece," they asked constantly, "your people needs you here"). The recruiters at the Western Wall and the bus station probably brought dozens of young people to the yeshiva each week. Only a few stayed longer than an hour. If the yeshiva did intend to brainwash, they were doing a poor job.

I remember wanting to write down exactly what was happening as I crossed the border into Orthodoxy, but for some reason I could not. I now realize that nothing was "happening"—no verbal abuse, no electrodes, no quarter-pounders—nothing an outsider could point to and say, "Aha! That's brainwashing!" Rather, each passing hour of those twelve days brought me in contact with more facets of Judaism. I was learning that my heritage was not simply a religion but a culture apart from Western culture, a history with sweep and majesty. Clearly there was more to being Jewish than my distant kinship with the Marx Brothers and Art Shamsky of the 1969 Mets. What I had known of Judaism before my arrival at the yeshiva was what my mother calls "chapter headings." Now I was reading the chapters themselves, and I liked what I was reading. To my mind, the rabbis at the yeshiva were not brainwashers. They were men with a mission—to teach people like me who had neutral or negative feelings toward Judaism how rich it really was; in short, to play the role of angel's advocate.

When I left the yeshiva twelve days after my arrival I had

undergone no transformation in my religious beliefs. What did I believe? Sometime in childhood I had latched onto the idea of monotheism and I never really doubted it. Although my family and friends believe otherwise, in twelve days I most definitely did not accept any one of the tenets that separate Orthodox Judaism from the religion's more liberal strains. But twelve days of questions and answers and classes and Sabbaths and events like a yeshiva wedding such as Frank described did serve as an indoctrination so thorough as to effect the kind of radical change implied by the dictionary definition of "brainwashing."

I left the yeshiva certain that I had to try Orthodoxy myself and test the claims that the rabbis made for it. Was observance of Jewish ritual the key to Judaism's future, the antidote to assimilation, the glue that would hold our people together, as the yeshiva's rabbis claimed? Would keeping the commandments make me a better person, son, brother, and one day husband and father? I had always been concerned, in an informal way, about how God expected people to behave or whether He had any expectations at all. Was the behavior taught in yeshiva what God wanted from people? From me? Were those young men in black slacks and white shirts really deciphering the blueprint of the universe? The rabbis' sense of mission had imbued me with a sense of mission—the urge to get answers to these Pressing Questions. In twelve days I had been transformed, by the force of argument and by the act of witnessing prayer and study and delight in both, transformed into a person who had to have answers. I was not committed to Orthodoxy—I was committed to experimenting with Orthodoxy, to testing the waters. And if this be brainwashing then I was brainwashed.

If there were no large events, no electrodes, no quarterpounders, what were the small things? What convinced me to postpone my last year of college, to give up graduating with my classmates and friends? The last eleven days of my initial stay at Ohr Samayach are as blurred in my memory as the first day remains clearly etched. When Marcel Proust was writing the *Remembrance of Things Past*, he would dip into his tea a madelaine, a sort of biscuit. The taste of the warm, wet biscuit would jog his memory and he would begin to write. Maybe I should try the same thing with some egg matzoh, or a chocolate macaroon.

My strongest memory from the twelve days is the realization that things which seemed so strange on my arrival seemed so natural by departure time. The Jewish Sabbath is a case in point. The basic idea behind the Sabbath is that you do your creative, remunerative work six days a week and on the seventh day you rest, just as God did when He was creating the world. We learn from the story of the Creation that the world is on a seven-day cycle. People who want to remain in harmony with the world therefore ought to respect the cycle and incorporate it into their lives. The Orthodox view the Sabbath as a chance to step back from one's pursuit of livelihood and gain a bit of perspective about life through quiet relaxation, meals with the entire family, and study and prayer.

If you have ever gone mountain climbing or skiing at very high elevations, you know that there exists a certain quiet, an absence of sound so total that you can feel it, a palpable silence. This silence cannot be described other than by saying that you become aware of all the things you do not hear—a neighbor's radio, a jet overhead, traffic, even the wind in the trees. It is a transforming silence, and later you remember the quiet on top of the mountain and how rested you felt. That first Sabbath afternoon in Jerusalem, the Sabbath of the portion of the spies, was the first time in my life that I heard that mountaintop silence in the middle of a city. It was incongruous, like meeting an old friend in a place where you had never known each other. "How fortunate these people are," I thought, "to enjoy this mountaintop silence one day out of every seven." As the next week at the yeshiva unfolded I looked forward to the return of that mountaintop silence. When it came back with the next Sabbath I greeted it as an old friend.

On that first Sabbath I was introduced to a student in his mid-twenties named Shmuel who helped me keep up with the morning prayer service by telling me when to turn pages. By the end of my twelve days in yeshiva, I had learned enough about the structure of the prayer service to be able to follow it on my own, another case of my growing accustomed to something which had been utterly foreign to my arrival. We heard the story of the spies chanted in Hebrew, and I felt the urge to study next week's portion in advance and in detail, as one might study an orchestral score to better enjoy a concert. The service seemed overlong but sincere. There was neither organ nor chorus, just one person leading and everyone else praying along in a sort of informal, almost disorganized piety. Except during the *Amidah*—the standing, silent prayer at the center of the service—people sat facing in all directions, each lost in his own thoughts and prayers. I had never seen a religious service where people did not all face the front as they sat.

After services Shmuel took me into Mea Shearim, the Orthodox neighborhood where Frank and I had eaten the challot on Thursday night, and where I was now fortunate enough to hear that mountaintop silence. Shmuel explained to me that we were going to eat at the house of a Hasid, a pious Jew devoted to a rebbe or community leader. Growing up, I had seen Hasidim in New York's diamond district. Some of them were my late grandfather's customers and suppliers in his diamond-importing business. I remembered those men as old and a bit stooped over, coming to my grandfather's office to show their goods. I was a little boy and I spoke no Yiddish, so I don't think I ever had a conversation with a Hasid. And today I would eat a Sabbath lunch with one. Imagine that.

On the way Shmuel offered a bit of religious protocol. "Don't speak while our host makes *Kiddush*, the blessing over the wine, then say amen and have a couple of sips; don't eat anything until you wash your hands in preparation for the *Motzi*, the blessing over the bread; and don't say anything between washing your hands and eating the slice of challah our host gives you." Shmuel said he would explain everything later. Our host was generous and friendly, and he seemed tolerant of my utter ignorance of religious practice. If I spent much of the meal staring at him, as I think I did, he pretended not to notice.

His appearance was unlike that of any other person I had ever known. He was a young man, perhaps around thirty. I had never seen such a young Hasid. He spoke unaccented English, a far cry from the Yiddish-speaking diamond merchants I remembered, but he spoke it through a beard so thick and bristly that he appeared to have no lips. Because it was the Sabbath, he wore a *shtreimel,* an oversized, triangular hat trimmed in beaver fur that noblemen once wore in Poland, a hat the size of a sombrero. He wore thin white socks beneath a gold-and-green *bekishe,* a delicately embroidered housecoat worn in honor of the holiness of the day. I certainly do not mean to insult my host of five years ago. But as I watched him speak normal English, appearing as he did with that bushy beard, the fur hat, the green-and-gold jacket, and the thin white socks, I remember thinking that I could not have been more surprised if I had met a tree who could speak proper English. But after twelve days which included conversations with other Hasidim, I had become accustomed even to their style of dress, unusual as it was to my assimilated eyes.

At that first meal, however, nothing could have been stranger than my host's appearance. Nothing, that is, until I asked him a few questions. Where was he from in America, I asked. Connecticut, he answered. To my mind, Connecticut meant wealthy, blonde-haired families zipping around New Canaan in Volvos, not Hasidic Jews. Connecticut always struck me as an elegant if somewhat studied place to live. Our host lived in a ramshackle house in Mea Shearim. I asked him when he was going back. His answer took me by surprise—he was never going back to Connecticut, except, perhaps, to visit his family. How could a person turn down Connecticut for a tiny home in Mea Shearim? Obviously, I had a lot to learn about the observant Jew's love of Jerusalem.

And in those days I learned a lot. I learned why it was not so odd for a person to prefer Jerusalem to any other place, even Fairfield County. I still do not understand why the yeshiva had sent me, a newcomer, to a home like that. Although I did not know it at the time, Orthodox Judaism spans a broad spectrum of behavior. More than one acceptable approach to a given custom or commandment may exist. For example, modesty leads some women to cover their hair after marriage with a kerchief, while some wear wigs, and some do not cover their hair at all. (This explains why the women I saw Thursday morning had their hair covered.) Yet each position is entirely defensible within the framework of Jewish law. Women choose whether and how to cover their hair based on the practice in the local community, their understanding of relevant Jewish law, and what makes them feel most comfortable. This comes as a surprise to virtually every baal teshuva—that Orthodoxy does not offer newcomers a single code of behavior to follow but forces them to make a bewildering number of decisions about virtually everything.*

On that first Sabbath I thought of Orthodoxy the way most people think of orthodoxies—that there was one right, best way of doing things, and that anyone who veered from the norm was either acting improperly or, in the case of my new yeshiva acquaintances, on the way toward reaching that standard. If Steven and Frank and Shmuel and I could only hold the course, one day we would all wear beaver-trimmed hats and green-and-gold housecoats on the Sabbath. "Well," I thought at the time, "if that's what Orthodox Judaism means, I'll try my best." But I could not picture myself in those thin white socks.

Forgive me for concentrating on appearances, but at that early stage it was all I knew. I was operating on the level of *pshat*, trying to grasp the surface meanings of things. One thing I saw at the home of the Connecticut Hasid was quite hard for me to understand, but I thought it would be improper to ask him about it. His wife had not introduced herself to me—had

---

*Many baalei teshuva solve this problem by adopting the customs and positions of the yeshiva that introduced them to observance. This applies not only to ritual practice but often to philosophy as well. For example, virtually all of the baalei teshuva with whom I spoke who attended a certain yeshiva in Israel expressed identical attitudes toward subjects as diverse as the Holocaust and the covering of women's hair.

not said a word to me, in fact. She seated herself at a smaller table, halfway to the kitchen door, leaving the larger table to her husband, Shmuel, and me. I knew from New York that Orthodoxy distinguished between men and women in many things. I couldn't wait to get Shmuel outside to ask him what was going on.

Since then I have eaten Sabbath and Yom Tov (Jewish holiday) meals in perhaps a hundred Orthodox homes, including the homes of some extremely pious people in the most pious of Orthodox neighborhoods, and in only one other family did a woman—an elderly widow—sit apart. During those first twelve days I learned what sorts of sacrifices the Orthodox way of life entailed—giving up nonkosher foods like bacon and shellfish (fried clams included), skipping the ballgame Saturday afternoon, getting up a little earlier to make time for prayer. None of these things seemed especially burdensome. But my largest stumbling block, and the hardest thing for most young, non-Orthodox people interested in their religion to accept, is the idea that in traditional Judaism men and women are not equal. Cheeseburgers I could do without, but I could not buy into a movement that seemed discriminatory. I spent a lot of time during those twelve days asking rabbis and students about it, and this is a good time to set down what I learned.

Men and women have obvious physical and biological differences, I was told. According to Orthodox Judaism, they have spiritual differences as well. The different roles Orthodoxy assigns men and women reflect those spiritual differences. People did not invent the spiritual differences any more than people invented the physical and biological ones. God did. Everything in Orthodoxy involving men doing one thing and women doing another springs from these basic premises.

The trouble with these premises, for most non-Orthodox Jews and non-Jews today, is that they presume far too much. Not everyone believes in God anymore, and even those that do are hardly likely to be comfortable with the notion that God does something that the United States Constitution forbids, that is, discriminating on the basis of sex. Orthodoxy makes no apologies for its position, I quickly learned. Many Orthodox people that I met over the last five years are so comfortable with the idea of religious distinctions based on spiritual differences that they do not understand the depth of feeling that surrounds this question in the non-Orthodox world.

Countless thoughtful Jewish young people concerned about understanding their spiritual heritage find the idea of sex-based distinctions so foreign and distasteful that it prevents them from having anything at all to do with Judaism. Some Orthodox people think that these young Jews use the issue as a pretext for avoiding Orthodox practice; that they are, in effect, hiding behind the issue so they don't have to give up cheeseburgers or premarital sex. Each side would be well advised to understand the position of the other, but face-to-face dialogue between Orthodox and non-Orthodox Jews on such delicate issues is all too rare. Baalei teshuva and their families and friends often want to know what these sex-based distinctions mean in day-to-day life. I will try to explain.

Baal teshuva yeshivas generally teach that the nature of men's souls is such that men need constant, daily physical reminders of the existence of God and of their role in life, which is to serve God in all that they do. While Jewish women are also expected to serve God, their spiritual nature is such that they do not need these constant physical reminders. Like many older cultures, Orthodox Judaism posits a public role for men and a private, home-based role for women. Now, I have met countless Orthodox women who work as doctors, lawyers, businesswomen, and even as veterinarians. The concept of sex-based differences is concerned primarily with ritual practice, not with career choice.

Sex roles in Orthodoxy thus proceed from two ideas: first, that men need constant reminders about God; and second, that men play the public role in life. These two ideas give rise to a class of rules in Jewish law called "time-contingent commandments," which are rules derived from the Bible or the Talmud that men must obey on a daily or weekly or monthly basis. For example, every weekday morning, every Jewish male over the age of thirteen must pray while wearing tefillin, that system of leather straps and boxes that I saw from the parapet window. The boxes contain parchments inscribed with paragraphs from the Bible. One binds a strap on one's arm in a manner symbolic of Abraham's binding his son Isaac on the altar and also symbolic of binding oneself to God. (I had never seen tefillin until that first morning at the yeshiva, but they are an integral part of life for Orthodox Jewish males.) Jewish law requires that one complete one's morning prayer within a certain, fixed period between sunrise and midmorning. Since there is a fixed, repetitive quality to the commandment of morning prayer, it falls into the category of "time contingent." Men must therefore pray in the mornings, but not women, because men need the repeated physical reminder about God and their being bound to God. According to Orthodox thinking, women do not need that reminder; therefore, they don't wear tefillin.

Friends and family of baalei teshuva often wonder how a person raised in a relatively egalitarian secular society can be comfortable with another decidedly sexist aspect of Jewish law—that women do not count in an Orthodox minyan (quorum for prayer) and that women cannot become Orthodox rabbis. According to Jewish law, ten people are necessary to conduct public prayer services. But not just any ten people, according to Orthodoxy—ten men. Why men and not women? The answer comes from the same two concepts we have already discussed—the public/private distinction and the idea of time-contingent commandments to remind men, who need reminding, about God. While most Orthodox Jewish legal authorities agree that women are obligated to pray in some form at least once a day, public prayer is a community function and therefore falls in the domain of men. Jewish law actually requires men to pray not once but three times a day—in the early morning, in the afternoon, and a third time after dark. Public prayer is a time-contingent commandment; therefore, men have the obligation and women do not. Orthodoxy therefore counts toward the minimum of ten for a minyan only people who bear that time-contingent obligation; namely, men.

Orthodox opposition to women as rabbis seems to be based partly on Jewish law and partly on social reasons—that it just would not feel right to have a woman as a community leader. This sort of thinking, of course, is very much at odds with the contemporary outlook.

"Equal rites" is the catchphrase that neatly sums up the pressure in all movements of Judaism—Orthodox, Conservative, Reform, and Reconstructionist—to allow women to enjoy the same status and responsibilities in Jewish law as men. Women are counted in and often lead Conservative services. Some Reform and Reconstructionist women wear a tallis, or prayer shawl, and tefillin when they pray. Women in Reform and some Conservative temples are called to the Torah during the service, an honor reserved to men in Orthodox sanctuaries, and in both movements women have been ordained as rabbis.*

It is not surprising that women should make such strides to "equal rites" in the more liberal branches of Judaism, because the frame of reference in those branches is the modern world and the modern outlook on the question of gender-based classifications. In American society we consider such classifications out of place at work or in applications for credit, and rightly so. If we do not permit sexual discrimination on the job or at the bank, so the reasoning goes, why should we permit it in the synagogue? This is why non-Orthodox Jews find the Orthodox position so out of touch with the times.

But the Orthodox, I learned, do not look at religion as one more aspect of life in America. For them the starting point is not American society's attitude toward women. Their frame of reference is what they believe God dictated to Moses and the Jewish people—that men and women have their spiritual differences, like it or not, and that religion must reflect them. Orthodoxy, moreover, finds these distinctions satisfying. It may seem hard to believe, but in five years of contact with

---

*Some Orthodox synagogues sanction "women's minyans"—parallel services run entirely by women. Many newly Orthodox women uncomfortable with Orthodoxy's separate seating for men and women find these services more to their taste. Such services have not found universal acceptance in Orthodox Judaism, though.

Orthodox men and women of all ages and places on the spectrum of religious practice, I rarely met anyone dissatisfied with the system that assigns men certain responsibilities and women others, or to put it another way, that gives men certain rights and denies those rights to women.

What follows may seem harder still to believe, and it comes as a shock to most baalei teshuva. Orthodox men still recite, every morning, a blessing thanking God because He "has not created me a woman." If your first reaction upon reading this is to slam the book closed in anger, I cannot blame you. Many people, especially those feminists who believe that Orthodox Judaism actually hates women, point to this blessing as proof. Certainly the blessing is the hardest thing to justify to non-Orthodox Jews, and it is by far the hardest thing for baalei teshuva—men and women alike—to justify to themselves. Most baalei teshuva either try not to think about the blessing or accept the explanation Orthodoxy offers, which is as follows: the prayer comes immediately after two other blessings, thanking God "who has not created me a non-Jew" and "who has not created me a slave." Taken together, says Orthodoxy, these three verses provide Jewish males with the chance to thank God for creating them with both the freedom and the obligation to fulfill all the commandments, even those from which women are exempt. (Women instead thank God "who has created me in accordance with His will.")

Look in a traditional prayer book and you will find the men's version in full-size type and the women's formula ("in accordance with His will") in small print or in the margin. The subtle message reinforces the message of the seating arrangement in Orthodox sanctuaries—the role of the woman in public prayer is essentially marginal, added on. My Jewish friends who knew about this blessing grilled me repeatedly: "How could you believe such a thing? How could you say it?" I answered that it disturbed me but it could not be wished away, and that in many ways women command more respect in Orthodox society than in the secular world. Pornography, rape, and other forms of violence against women are not products of Orthodox

Jewish culture. Still, my response could not diminish the intensity of feeling that this verse provoked in my friends. One of my yeshiva acquaintances went so far as to get special permission from his rabbi not to say the blessing. It bears repeating that baalei teshuva do not necessarily accept all of the teachings of Orthodoxy from the moment they sign on.

During those first twelve days I heard repeatedly something that my later experience bore out—if you take any element of Orthodoxy out of context, it seems hard to justify. But if you view it within the entire system of Orthodox life, you see that it makes sense as part of the system. My gut feeling toward Orthodoxy's sex-based stereotyping was the product of a secular upbringing and a liberal education—I didn't like the sex-based distinctions, I didn't fully accept the justifications Orthodoxy offered, and I didn't think I could come to believe them. Even today, five years later, I am still not comfortable with the idea of separate synagogue seating and no role in the service for women. I wish that Orthodoxy would relent, at least on this issue, because it is the greatest obstacle between thoughtful young Jewish people and their faith. But I'm not holding my breath. Many baalei teshuva, when pressed on the subject, do not accept completely these gender-based distinctions. Family and friends are advised not to assume that the baal teshuva in their life has suddenly become a misogynist.

Chapter 6

Now I Look Like a Unicorn

As the twelve days wore on, I continued to attend the classes in Bible, Talmud, and "Structures" and sat in on some lectures on prayer and on the Jewish calendar. Out of class, I buttonholed rabbis and advanced students and sat late into the night in the beit midrash, the central study room, listening and learning. There was always an answer to my questions. Most of the yeshiva students and even some of the rabbis, after all, had been asking the same things only a few months or a few years before. When I had trouble accepting what I was hearing, I was reminded that some aspects of Judaism are hard to understand when taken out of context but make sense when viewed as part of the system. Revelation followed relevation during the twelve days; Judaism slowly took shape before my eyes.

What did I learn? In and out of classrooms I was told that there is nothing in the Torah or Talmud that contradicts the theory of evolution; that biblical creation, even if taken literally, and evolution can be harmonized without doing violence to either religion or science. I learned that Judaism enforces its notion of praising God for all things that happen to a person, good and bad, through a complex system of blessings. There are special blessings at mealtimes—different blessings for different kinds of food. There are blessings to make upon seeing a wonder of nature—the ocean, a rainbow, the first budding tree in springtime. There is even a blessing to be said after going to the bathroom. One is not blessing the food or the ocean or the plumbing fixtures, I learned. Through the blessings one thanks

God, who is responsible for nourishing us, for providing us with a physical world of great power and beauty, and who is after all responsible for the design of our digestive system. Sometimes people speak disdainfully of a "higher consciousness" that religion supposedly helps people attain. What I admired in Judaism was its drive toward simple consciousness, an awareness on the part of people who believe in God that God's hand can be observed everywhere, and its structure—those myriad blessings—to bring that simple consciousness home to everyone.

I learned how to put on tefillin, the leather straps and boxes. It happened this way: one morning, after the prayer service, Shmuel looked at me and asked in his tentative manner—he was always afraid that he would go too far, "Mordechai," using my Hebrew name, "would you . . . like to put on tefillin?" "Well, why not," I thought—I was committed to experimenting, and I couldn't postpone tefillin forever. After all, Jewish males had been wearing them for thousands of years, and, according to tradition, God at Mount Sinai had told Moses how to design them.

I remember thinking how silly tefillin looked; the box that rests on the forehead at one's hairline makes men resemble unicorns with stubby, black horns. Shmuel first gave me the part that went on the arm, a leather box on a strap that fits over one's bicep, symbolic of subjugating one's physical strength and carnal desires to God's service, and then he showed me how to wrap the strap around my forearm. Then he told me to lean forward and he placed the second part around my head, another leather box resting above my forehead, symbolizing the subjugation of one's capacity to reason to a Being who can never be understood through reason. I remember thinking, "Now I look like a unicorn with a small black horn, too." I was also frightened to be wearing tefillin. Would I always have to wear them now? Would I always want to? I felt as though I had put my head in a yoke that I had skillfully avoided for twenty years.

There is one more thing I remember thinking as I bent my

head forward to receive the tefillin. For a moment I was the prince in a fairy tale, a prince who had avoided the throne of his father, the king, all his life—until that morning, when I bent my head forward to receive my crown of thin, soft leather, a black diadem concealing biblical parchment. I had taken my rightful place among my people. I had arrived.

I also saw celebrations at the yeshiva. One of the students announced his engagement one morning after prayers. Actually, a friend of his announced it while the yeshiva students were taking off their tefillin and getting ready for breakfast. The young men were jubilant. Rabbis and students—two hundred men—snake-danced and sang down a rapidly cleared path in the beit midrash. We sang and danced for a quarter of an hour, sometimes to wordless melodies and sometimes to songs which I later learned are only sung at an engagement announcement or a wedding. "And again there shall be heard in the streets of Judah and the corners of Jerusalem the voice of gladness and the voice of joy, the voice of the groom and the voice of the bride." (That's the translation; in Hebrew it sounds much smoother.) We danced and stamped and sang while the early-morning Jerusalem sun lit our faces through the parapet windows. The dancing stopped amid a chorus of "Mazel tov!" and "Soon by you!" which is what people tell each other at such moments.

Another celebration: another of the students was getting married that night, and all the rabbis and students were invited. We packed ourselves five to a taxi and headed to one of the hotels in downtown Jerusalem. The wedding was just as Frank had described at the bar that first night—lots of dancing, and lots of checking out of the opposite sex. (No brazen introductions, though, no seeking of telephone numbers— everything had to be cleared through a go-between first.)

The men danced with the men, the women with the women, in keeping with Orthodox custom. We spun ourselves in mad circles; arms over each other's shoulders, we made ourselves giddy and dizzy. I found my arm around the back of the registrar, my Talmud instructor, as we danced. I felt release and I felt acceptance; I wanted all these strangers to dance one day at my wedding.

A third celebration came two nights later. The wife of the rabbi whose prayer class I was attending had just given birth to a son. The yeshiva community was invited to a *Shalom Zachor*, a Friday evening gathering in honor of the newborn. That Friday afternoon I helped Yoel, the father, bring chairs from all over the neighborhood into his home, a small two-bedroom apartment in a modern complex behind the yeshiva. The living room was jammed with chairs, but they were all needed, as it turned out.

After Sabbath dinner that Friday night most of the yeshiva showed up with their wives and children, thirty at a time. The *roshei yeshiva*—the deans—arrived early and were given seats of honor at the dining room table. The room would fill and one of the rabbis would give a brief discourse on the Torah portion of the week, or on something in the Talmud, and would tie it to the many fine qualities of the baby's parents and the high hopes the community had for the baby, always ending with the phrase, *Hu yichanes le-Torah, le chupah ulimasim tovim*—"He should enter into the study and practice of Torah, the marriage canopy, and good deeds," a formula I thought rather far-sighted. The assembled would shout "Amen! L'chayim!" and would all down a shot of scotch or bourbon or wine and sing something at once religious and raucous.

The guests would then troop out, the next thirty would come in, and another rabbi would be off and running with some scriptural clue to the baby's future and maybe a word about the lovely grandparents, also at the table, who had flown in from Ohio to be present at the birth. More amens and l'chayims, more toasts, and more singing, and then the next group would come storming in.

I had asked a lot of questions in the eight days between my arrival and the *Shalom Zachor*, but there was one thing I could not find courage to ask about. My question was whether liquor was kosher. You try it. There you are in an Orthodox yeshiva, and people are praying and learning Talmud all day long, and you want to ask about booze. I could give up cheeseburgers, but alcohol was something else. Fortunately for me, I found an answer at that Friday night celebration. For there on a silver tray were Johnnie Walker Black, and Jack Daniels, and Gordon's Gin, and other old friends, and I thought to myself, this was a religion that I wanted into.

All liquor except most wines and wine-based products like brandy is kosher, I later learned. Wines are kosher only if processed by Jews or under Jewish supervision, for two reasons, both of which date back centuries. First, in ancient times, certain pagan religious practices often included pouring libations to the gods. Jewish law forbade the drinking of wine which had been used or might have been used for such purposes. Second, wine was the single most popular social beverage in those days. The rabbis feared that drinking wine with non-Jews would lead to getting drunk with non-Jews, which could lead to illicit contact with non-Jews, which in turn could lead to intermarriage, shotgun style and otherwise, with non-Jews. Judaism has rarely been a proselytizing religion; even today, parents and grandparents put a premium bordering on the irrational (to their children's minds) on marrying within the faith. The ban on Gentile wine was an early and successful fence against intermarriage.*

(One day in yeshiva a few years later, the subject of other drinks came up as four of us sat with our rabbi waiting for a latecomer to arrive to a Talmud class. We asked why there was no similar ban on vodka and Scotch and other forms of hard liquor, since today they share wine's role as a social beverage. The rabbi answered that the lack of unity among the various factions within Orthodoxy makes new decisions and bans impossible, but, in his opinion, if the leaders of the different

---

*The different branches of Judaism, unsurprisingly, hold different attitudes toward the conversion of non-Jews. The traditional view, still accepted by the Orthodox, is to wonder why anyone would want to join a people so downtrodden in history. The most usual setting for conversion today is when a Jew wishes to marry a non-Jew. Orthodoxy demands the highest level of compliance with Jewish law from its converts; other movements expect a serious commitment to Judaism that does not necessarily express itself in terms of adherence to Jewish law.

groups ever do sit down to discuss the matter, Johnnie Walker will go the way of Cabernet Sauvignon. Marijuana too, for that matter. Only four students heard the rabbi's off-the-cuff remark about grass, but by nightfall not a student in the yeshiva had not heard it. Bad news travels fast.)

Well, there I was, ten of the Twelve Days gone by, my head filled with impressions—the L-shaped blocks of Talmud text; the high priest's mother spreading cheer among ancient manslaughterers; blessings for falafel, cherry trees, and on leaving the men's room; tefillin; dancing around the yeshiva floor and the dance floor of a Jerusalem hotel; green-and-gold bekishes and beaver-trimmed shtreimels; mountaintop silences in a city on Saturday afternoons; thundering sermons and midnight Q and A sessions; I was fascinated and I was hooked.

"I hear you're going to Greece," other students still said to me. "Your people needs you here." I often wondered whether the yeshiva administration knew of the coercion that students put on other students, some of the strongest proselytizers having been at the yeshiva only a few weeks themselves. The rabbis also tried to talk me into staying but I was not interested. I would be back after the summer and not before then. I asked everyone I met for recommendations of books to buy and bring along to Greece, and I took along a small cache of books about Judaism.

How did my parents react to my postponing graduation for two years? I expected them to resist because I knew They'd Never Understand. Resist? They went wild. They thought they had lost their son and that their son had lost his mind. Not come home? Three weeks before I had been a normal college kid and now I wanted to spend two years reading Talmud, of all things. I had never before given them cause for serious alarm, with the exception of a few too-late nights out with friends in high school. Nothing I had ever done could have prepared them for this. I will never forget the fear, the alarm in their voices, and how stubborn and high-handed I was over the telephone. I do not believe that I had the smugness of a convert to a cause. I was, quite simply, too excited by all I had seen and learned to think clearly.

Over the telephone I asked them to suspend judgment until they received a long letter I had written explaining what I had seen in the yeshiva that made me want to stay. They were adamant, they were scared; they pleaded, they threatened. I could not be budged. After all, I had seen it written in the Talmud—in the Talmud, mind you—that parents who oppose their children's study of Torah will eventually come to accept it and delight in it. I listened to my poor panicked parents and I thought, "Maybe you don't like it now, but you will."

Today, five years later, I look back on those telephone calls and I cannot help but be upset at myself for putting my parents through such an ordeal. I suspect that many parents of baalei teshuva undergo similar experiences. Could I really have expected my parents to say, "That's fine, dear, have a good two years at the yeshiva, and we'll see you later?" But just as quickly, I wonder whether I am being too harsh on myself. I was only twenty; I was fascinated by all that I was learning, and I was flattered by all the attention I received at the yeshiva as a raw recruit. I was determined, though, and late in the evening of a June 18 five years ago, I said goodbye to my new friends and took my borrowed tefillin, my stack of books and a small black yarmulke I had bought from an elderly Hasid in the back of the beit midrash, and I took a taxi to the airport. The long-distance debate with my parents remained unresolved, but the Twelve Day Wonder was on his way.

Chapter 7

Nude Beaches Suddenly Irreconcilable

The yeshiva had an unassailable point, I had to admit. However much I had resented the hard sell from both students and faculty ("Why go to Greece? Your people needs you here!"), the rocky Greek islands were hardly fertile soil in which baalei teshuva, newly religious Jews, can take root. Athens and Rhodes, an island near the Turkish shore, had once been home to large Jewish populations, but after the Second World War only a few families remained. A convert to Orthodoxy (or to anything) obviously stands a better chance of remaining religious if the initial exposure to the group lasts longer than twelve days. The yeshiva probably wrote me off when I left, and they most likely also wrote off the expensive tefillin I had borrowed. Gone to Greece, gone for good.

I did not feel that way. I welcomed the chance to get away from the yeshiva and think through, on my own, all that I had seen and heard. I was committed to a moderate level of religious practice—not eating shellfish and nonkosher meat; not doing schoolwork on a Saturday; davening, or praying, three times a day, wearing tefillin while I prayed in the mornings; and, most obvious to the outside world, wearing the yarmulke. (Of course, until then, I had never equated what one ate, or when one studied, with spirituality. This is an adjustment for all baalei teshuva, one that Jews born Orthodox often find hard to understand, because they grew up accustomed to thinking in these terms.) Greece was a good place to try on Orthodoxy because virtually no one I knew was going to be there. The Jews spent forty years in the desert when they first accepted the Torah, living apart from the rest of civilization while adjusting to the new rules. I would spend six weeks in Poros, a small town on the edge of the Peloponnese, two hours by hydrofoil south of Athens, doing the same thing.

On a symbolic level, the ancient Greek world I had studied at college was diametrically opposed to everything Orthodoxy stood for. The Greeks worshipped the perfection of the human body. Jews do not consider the body, at least, the male body, complete without a physical reminder of the person's entrance into the covenant—the *brit milah,* or ritual circumcision. The ancient Greeks thought Jewish circumcision was barbaric (as some people think today). Our God has qualities we strive to emulate; the Greek gods' Olympian capacity for lust, intrigue, pleasure, and publicity makes ancient mythology read like *People* magazine.

Another point of difference: the highpoint of Jewish worship is the *Amidah,* or silent prayer. Jews pray silently to let the heart communicate directly with God even though the person is standing in a crowded room. According to Euripides, the Greek playwright, the ancient Greeks also prayed in a whisper—but only so that the gods to whom the prayer was not directed would not overhear it, become jealous, and interfere with the supplicant and his or her chosen god.

One last contrast: remains of Greek temples today pose uniformly and dramatically white against the deep blue sky, much like New England churches. But the Greeks painted those austere-looking temples in colors so bright that they would seem garish to the modern eye. The ancient Greeks stood not inside but in front of their temples when they prayed, their eyes dazzled by the colors. Those brightly painted columns stand in sharp contrast to the monochromaticism of the dark-paneled beit midrash, the central study room in the yeshiva, filled with young men in dark slacks and white shirts. We are not peacocks, the message says, we are not here to glorify our bodies through fancy clothing or our house of study through pastel colors. We are here to do solemn work, the colors say.

Forget symbolism. Modern Greece was no place for a baal teshuva. What did the yeshiva know about the nude beaches, the Greek wine, the calamari? I knew plenty—I had been to Greece before. For most American backpackers in Europe, Greece is the Promised Land, well earned after patient sight-seeing at the Tower of London, the Louvre, the sparkling dullness of Geneva, and the confusion and heat that is Italy in the summer. I should recount something that happened on an earlier trip to Greece. I had come to Corfu the year before on an overnight ferry, down the Adriatic coast from Yugoslavia. On the boat I met two young Americans from California who were bicycling their way across Europe and who were thoroughly disgusted with their travels. They had seen plenty, they said, but they hadn't met a woman in five weeks. The first morning at Corfu I caught up with one of them, stark naked, on the beach. Beside him on the sand was an equally naked, abso-lutely stunning young blonde-haired woman.

"Michael, this is Karen. Karen, Michael. Karen's from Swe-den."

Nice to meet you.

I'll be honest. Completing my ancient Greek major was only a partial motive for returning to Greece. I wanted more retsina (resin-flavored Greek wine), and more calamari, and more olives, and more Swedish women on the nude beaches. And there I was, back in Greece, but the joke was on me. Calamari wasn't kosher, nor was retsina, and nude beaches could simply not be reconciled with strict Orthodox practice.

And yet, in a backhanded sort of way, I owed my exposure to Orthodoxy to my Greek studies. It happened this way: as a sophomore at Amherst I took a course in classical Greek civilization which led to my declaring a major in Greek. I needed two courses that summer to complete the major, and I found a program in Greece that offered those courses. Now,

Orthodox Judaism believes that people have free will and choose their own actions. This I learned during my twelve days in yeshiva. Yet God, paradoxically, has foreknowledge of what those choices will be. There is obviously a tension between free will and determinism, yet Judaism posits that they exist side by side. The Hebrew term is *hashgacha pratit*, or "concern with the small details," which is what Judaism believes God has. During those first days back in Greece, I wondered whether God really was intimately concerned with the little things in our lives and whether He really did give us direction through them. Could I have been following some divine script on my path via the Amherst College classics department and the nude beaches of Corfu to the yeshiva door? I wondered.

Hashgacha pratit, concern for the small details. I had taken a small room with a balcony overlooking the Heraklion fruit market on Crete. From my porch I watched the tourists and the local people conduct business in the hot sun, and I wrote four aerograms—three to my would-have-been roommates and one to the college registrar—informing them that I was not coming back to Amherst in the fall. Those were hard aerograms to write; yet, to my mind, it had to be this way. The yeshiva had convinced me of the importance of understanding Judaism. I was intoxicated with the idea of Judaism, and I wanted to grasp it with both hands.

Hashgacha pratit, concern for the small details. The previous summer, the summer I discovered the beaches of Corfu, my father moved out of the house for several weeks in an attempt to keep my parents' marriage alive by giving each partner a little time apart. He moved back before the summer ended. Every time the telephone rang the following year, my junior year at college, the year I began to study Greek, part of me feared that this was the telephone call to tell me that the marriage was over.

The call never came; at least not during the school year. Two days after I left Israel, six hours after I met the people with whom I would spend six weeks, studying ancient Greek language and culture, the call came through. It was past midnight; I was drinking coffee in the bar of the hotel where we were staying. It was my mother; they had decided to divorce.

I was shocked, of course, and saddened, and I felt bad because my moment of rebellion—my desire to delay graduation and study Judaism in Jerusalem—had come about when my parents were least able to cope. My family and most of my friends thought the relationship between the divorce and my infatuation with Orthodoxy was that of cause and effect. I did not believe that at the time. After all, I had left the yeshiva, committed to a year's study there before I knew of the breakup.

Hashgacha pratit. I have never been comfortable with the concept of determinism, of things being *bashert*, to use the Yiddish word for "preordained." (Some Orthodox people who become engaged refer to their fiancé as their *bashert*.) I suppose I had been brought up to believe that you make your own luck and have no one to thank, or blame, but yourself. But if they were right about *bashert*, about *hashgacha pratit*, about that invisible hand, I had to admit that Orthodoxy had come into my life at a time when I most needed something to turn to. I might have found my way to the yeshiva at some other time. But why right then, when an important part of my life—my parents' marriage—had finally dissolved? Why then?

The divorce had two effects on me, but only one was clear at the time. I remember thinking that my parents' breakup was another arrow in Orthodoxy's quiver, another good argument for attempting to live differently from the way most people live in America, because something bad was happening in American society. The marriages of many of my friends' parents had ended before we finished high school.

Rabbis at the yeshiva had argued that America takes authentic Jewishness away from Jews and gives nothing but empty, material things in return. The Hebrew word for "rain" is *geshem*, and rain is considered a blessing, an obvious connection for a once-agrarian people. The Yiddish word for "material things" is *goshmeis*, which is really a corruption of the Hebrew word for "worldliness" but is homiletically sometimes said to be a plural form of *geshem*. Like rain, material things are a blessing—but not in surfeit. America is drowning in material things, said the rabbis, and the things that matter—love, marriage, family, community—are swept away. My parents' divorce made me think that perhaps the Orthodox were on to something. They represented a finger in the dike, a way to come in from the rain.

What I did not realize at the time was my vulnerability. Had my roommate Steven gone to the Hare Krishna and not the yeshiva, I doubt that I would have succumbed. But the yeshiva had two things going for it—timing, and my previous interest in its product. From the time I stood in the temple library gazing at that secret-filled L-shaped block of text, from the time, as a little boy, I stood solemnly beside my grandfather in his Orthodox synagogue on West 95th Street in Manhattan, pretending that I could read Hebrew, I always wanted to be a part of Judaism; at that moment, in a bar in Heraklion at half past midnight, learning by telephone that my parents' marriage was no more, I needed it as well.

While in Greece I had no contact with Orthodoxy—I did not see another observant Jew during my entire stay. Mine was, in effect, a Judaism without Jews. Had an Orthodox Jew happened onto Poros, the location of the study program, he would have been surprised by what he saw. People wearing yarmulkes do not eat even fish cooked in nonkosher pots, and they certainly do not make *Kiddush,* the Friday night blessing over the wine, on retsina, the Greek resin wine I remembered from Corfu. But if that person had asked me about my commitment to traditional Judaism, he would have been quite surprised by my utter captivation with the subject. I admit now that part of my fervor was fueled by the divorce. But the bulk of it was genuine affection for my complicated religion.

Two life crises in two weeks—the conversion and the divorce. I wanted to come home, but my family was adamant that I stay in Greece. They believed, and rightly so, that I could not join together what time had put asunder, and that I might as well not throw my summer away. So I stayed, with my yarmulke and tefillin. The group met for the first time that afternoon in Heraklion. We would sightsee together for a few days among the ancient Minoan palaces of Crete and then take an overnight boat to Athens and a quick, two-hour boat trip down the Peloponnesian coast to Poros, a lush, tiny island that Henry Miller made famous in *The Colossus of Maroussi*.

I suppose I should have felt shell-shocked by the sudden changes in my life, but the Greek islands in the summer are so beautiful that it is hard to feel sorry for oneself there. The palaces of Crete were splendid, our guide able, and the group seemed friendly enough. When the boat pulled into Poros on a bright, sunny morning in late June, the pillbox-shaped houses of the town, whitewashed or painted in pastels, glowed with color, and their reflection shimmered in the harbor. This was no place for self-pity.

We stayed two and three to a room and took our meals in a small hotel on the Peloponnesian mainland, across a narrow strait from the island of Poros. I arose early each morning to put on my tefillin and run through as much of the morning prayer service as I could in thirty or forty minutes. My roommate slept as I prayed. I remember panicking one morning because I had forgotten overnight how to put on my borrowed tefillin. The process is rather complicated, I had only been doing it for a few weeks, and no one on Poros could have reminded me. But after a few fretful minutes I finally remembered how, and the crisis passed.

The atmosphere of the program was so casual, compared to the serious world of the beit midrash. It was also pleasant to be back in a class with women after the all-male yeshiva. The Aristophanes class consisted of three of us sitting at a decaying Ping-Pong table on the grounds of a villa, studying *The Birds*, an ancient Greek comedy. Back to the hotel for lunch and preparation for my afternoon class, a tutorial on another play. The late afternoons were for homework and the occasional beach excursion; no, sad to report, not to nude beaches.

The others in the group mostly ignored my yarmulke, as self-conscious as I was about it. I found myself much more aware, at times painfully aware, of my behavior. I felt as though I was observant Judaism's representative and that people would judge Judaism by the way I carried myself. As I later learned, this is one of the ideas behind the yarmulke. Another reason for wearing it is that it reminds the wearer that there is something above him, namely God, and that he is a servant of that higher being.

There was a third reason, one with which I was never comfortable. The word *Zion*, which evokes thoughts of Jerusalem, the land of Israel, the Jewish people, and thus of Judaism, is very similar to the Hebrew word for "sign." A yarmulke on the head of a person walking down the street is a sign, a reminder to all around him that there is a God out there somewhere. Now, my ideas about religion came from a society where spirituality was not something for public consumption. I was always ill at ease among my born-again Christian college friends when they wore large crucifixes around their necks. The concept of keeping one's religiosity a private matter is not foreign to Judaism, despite yarmulkes. In Yiddish there is an expression, "If he's so righteous why do I know about it?", meaning, how genuine is a person who insists on telling the world of his piety? But you have to wear a yarmulke anyway.

Not until nineteenth-century Germany and the Reform movement did some rabbis go bareheaded at synagogue services, imitating Lutheran ministers. Orthodoxy did not give up the idea of yarmulkes as a baseline test of religious commitment until Jews came in large numbers to America, where the yarmulke simply did not fit in on the job. Today there is a renaissance of yarmulke-wearing among younger Jews who have no qualms about identifying publicly with their people. This reminds me of seeing a group of American teenagers sightseeing in Jerusalem in 1982. They all wore T-shirts that said "I'm proud to be Jewish," but their pride did not manifest itself in a desire to wear a yarmulke, something I could easily understand. In Jerusalem it is very easy to wear a yarmulke, since so many other people have them on. On Poros it was a little harder, but I was committed to my experiment with Orthodoxy, and since Orthodoxy meant yarmulke, I wore it.

Actually, only two people asked me about it. One was a classics student from Wellesley named Pamela. Not long after the program began, Pamela's grandfather suffered a severe heart attack. We took turns that summer accompanying one another across the strait in the little ferry boat to the telephone bureau where we would call home and catch up with the latest in bad news from America. The battle continued to rage over where I would spend the coming year. Pamela's grandfather alternately worsened and improved. Nightly we took solace from the Greek coffee and galaktabourikos—a custard pastry made from milk—served at the outdoor cafes along the waterfront.

I gave up my plan of immediate yeshiva study after about three weeks of fighting with my family. I agreed to come back and finish college at the end of the summer. My greatest fear over returning to America was that my experiment with Orthodoxy would bend and snap under the strain of college life. But I realized that I had stared down the challenge of nude beaches and calamari, and, to paraphrase Frank Sinatra, if I could make it in Poros as an Orthodox Jew I could make it anywhere. Meanwhile, on beaches, at cafes while sipping sweet Greek coffee, on the porch of my room overlooking the strait of Poros, I made my way through the pile of books about Judaism that I had bought in Jerusalem. The yeshiva deans, had they known, would have been delighted.

(According to Levin family legend, as the ocean liner that brought my great-grandmother to America neared New York, her sons took her *sheitel*—her wig—from her head and threw it overboard. Some very Orthodox women cover their hair with a wig out of modesty, just as the women I saw on my first morning in Jerusalem covered their hair with handkerchiefs. "That was for the old country, ma!" her sons said. "This is America!" As I sat and read those books it dawned on me that they had thrown a lot more than a sheitel into the Atlantic.)

Our last night in Poros was the twenty-seventh of July. The group was to visit Olympia and other sites of antiquity, but a fast-day on the Jewish calendar—Tisha B'Av—was drawing near. I was curious as to how the day was marked in Jerusalem. Wandering through Olympia, even on an empty stomach, did not seem the right way to spend Tisha B'Av. My commitment to understanding Orthodox Judaism had survived seven weeks on a Greek island. I had foregone the shellfish, the lamb, and all the other pleasures of Greece in the summer. Now I would go back to the yeshiva for a two-week visit, in time for the fast-day of Tisha B'Av, and attempt to reduce further my vast ignorance about my heritage.

"I wanted to stay out of circulation long enough until my Jewish identity was strong enough to make it in the 'real world' outside the Yeshiva," I wrote my family as I capitulated in mid-July. "The last three weeks have taught me that it is strong enough. What is important is that I live as a Jew and not give up my other obligations—school, family—in the process. In that case it makes much more sense for me to finish Amherst and then choose the best atmosphere for studying Judaism—Yeshiva University? Jewish Theological Seminary?—for the two years after graduation."

The yeshiva had stressed the importance of family during the Twelve Days, and it made no sense to abandon my family for the yeshiva's womblike protection when I was most needed at home. When I recall how swept away I was by my exposure to traditional Judaism, I am surprised that I had enough sense to make the decision to come home. My family and I struck a deal: as long as I came home and finished college on time, they would give me some financial help the following year, if I still wanted to return to yeshiva.

Another paragraph from the same letter reveals just how seriously I took my new connection with Judaism: "There seems to be a parallel between my situation and one in *Bereishis* [Genesis]. I feel as though I have been asked to sacrifice the greatest pleasure I was to possess—living with my roommates, and graduating with my class. As you know, after great thought I agreed to give those things up in order to study the religion, and then at the last minute it turns out that my sacrifice was not the question, but what mattered was my willingness to make the sacrifice." I saw myself not merely as a rank-and-file observant Jew but as Abraham himself, the knife-blade pointed at the throat of that which I held most dear, until I heard the angel's voice. Maybe I was taking the whole thing a little too seriously.

Chapter 8

Bringing Home the Bacos

On the plane back to New York I was seated next to two nuns. I wondered if there were sections in the aircraft not just for smoking and nonsmoking passengers but also for religious and nonreligious. During the flight I read an article in *Time* magazine about religion in America—a survey indicated that young people no longer publicly expressed what religious feeling they had. Look out, *Time* magazine, I'll show you religious feeling.

My father met me at the airport in New York, and we both had adjustments to make: his son was wearing a yarmulke in public; my father was no longer married to my mother, and no longer lived at home. Now came the task of adjusting to living as an observant Jew in a nonobservant home and at a school that had no observant Jewish students or teachers. I wondered how long I would last. Once again I was in the same position as that of every baal teshuva whose initial contact with Orthodoxy comes while he or she is away from home. Reentry is a delicate phase in the process of transformation, a phase often complicated by the inability of baalei teshuva to express all that they saw and felt which contributed to the decision to experiment with Orthodoxy.

My greatest obstacle was my own ignorance of Jewish law. Three weeks in yeshiva is not long enough to learn how to observe the Sabbath, or the laws about kosher food, or anything. More important, I did not know anything about the practical side of observant Judaism—how Orthodox people who function in modern society strike a balance between their religion and American culture. I did not know about some of the key adjustments and compromises that make Orthodoxy possible in American life.

We should define our terms for a moment. I have been using *traditional*, *Orthodox*, and *observant* as synonymous designations for people who accept the basic ideas of Judaism—that there is a God, that He gave laws and commandments to Moses, and that it is still important for Jews to live by those laws, or at least by the interpretations of the mainstream of Jewish rabbinical thinking over the centuries.* I have tried not to use the word *religious* as a synonym for "observant" even though *religious* is the word that Orthodox people use to describe one another. I do not use it because there are, of course, many people who do not observe Jewish law who are religious, and, sad to say, many people who are observant but give no sign of any religious feeling. One might note that people from Orthodox homes who give up Jewish ritual practice are still referred to as "religious," along "prodigal son" lines, I suppose.

The Hebrew term for "Jewish law" is *halacha*, which could be translated as "the way to go." After two thousand years without a central religious authority to make laws for all Jews, there have developed a variety of acceptable ways to perform many commandments. (There are even two different ways to make tefillin. Some extremely observant people actually wear one set while they pray and then take them off and put on the other set for a brief period of time.) Nothing could have been more confusing to a neophyte like me. Orthodox people base decisions about how or whether to perform any given custom on three things I did not have—what their family did, what their religious school taught, and what they like to do, based on personal experience. For me, the "way to go" was less of a straight path and more of a minefield.

The laws about some things were clear, though. Like fried clams. Just as Greece changed in the twelve days I was away,

*Conservative Judaism is a bit more flexible in its application of ancient law to modern times. Reform and Reconstructionist Judaism believe that Jewish law should guide but not control decisions about practice and belief.

so New York changed during the summer. I could no longer eat in my favorite restaurants, like La Potagerie, a soup and salad place on Fifth Avenue in the Forties, and Wo Hop, a basement restaurant in Chinatown where taxi drivers would eat and pay for the food out of large wads of one dollar bills. I mourned the loss of my restaurants, but there was nothing to be done—they weren't kosher, and I was.

What is all this about kosher food? Why do people care about it, and what does it mean? The sources for the laws of kashrut—what is and isn't kosher—are found in two places. One is the first five books of the Bible, which Orthodox Jews call the Written Torah. The other source is the Oral Law, the tradition that began, Orthodox Jews believe, when God spoke to Moses at Mount Sinai, later codified in the Talmud. Some of the biblical prohibitions have already been mentioned—the rule against mixing meat and milk, for example, which gives rise to the curiosity about cheeseburgers. Clams, and all shellfish are not kosher, because the Bible says that only fish with fins and scales can be kosher.

The word kosher, by the way, does not mean "clean" or even "Jewish." It means "proper," in the sense that if you perceive yourself as belonging to a group whose members are committed to acknowledging God through all of their actions, including even their eating habits, then certain foods may be proper to eat as preparation for that role and others not.

Kosher meat, for example, is a two-step process. First, the animal itself must be kosher. The Bible requires that an animal must chew its cud and have cloven hoofs if it is to be kosher. Second, it must be slaughtered in accordance with the laws of kosher slaughtering. Some observant Jews, particularly those baalei teshuva for whom Orthodoxy was an outgrowth of vegetarianism, do not eat meat at all. Others will eat it only on Sabbaths and holidays, when there is a biblical requirement to feast and make merry, since meat and wine are traditional symbols of feasting. There are remarkable arguments within the Talmud and elsewhere over whether eating meat is justifiable at all. (These arguments predate the discovery of cholesterol—they began long before red meat got such a bad name in respectable society.)

The laws regulating kosher food are quite complex, and thus there were several reasons why I could not eat in nonkosher restaurants. Chief among them, of course, the ingredients used in preparing a kosher meal must themselves be kosher, and you can only be sure of this in a restaurant that follows all the rules of kashrut. In addition, the utensils used to prepare and serve kosher food must never come into contact with non-kosher foods. Some Orthodox people, particularly those in the business world, make certain compromises on kashrut observance outside the home and will have salad, or fish, or coffee, in nonkosher restaurants. Drinking in nonkosher restaurants presents much less of a problem from the point of view of Jewish law. (I should note here that becoming kosher was a difficult adjustment for me. Although I gave up nonkosher meat after the Twelve Days, it took a full year before I was in full compliance.)

We have talked about meat and fish, but there is much more to kashrut than that. Take cheese. Most cheese is made with rennet, a starter that comes from the stomach lining of cows. This gets one into trouble with the rule against mixing meat and milk. Observant people will only eat cheese made from a chemical enzyme starter. How can a person tell whether the cheese comes from rennet or enzymes? The answer is on the label. Virtually every packaged food that is kosher carries a little symbol called a *hekhsher,* or guarantee of kashrut. Various rabbis and large Jewish organizations supervise the preparation of the foods and place their hekhsherim, their symbols, on the product.

The most frequently seen hekhsher is the "O-U," a letter *U* in a circle, standing for "Orthodox Union," the largest Orthodox rabbinical organization. Other supervisory agencies have their own stylized symbols, and sometimes the imprimatur of a particular rabbi is given by printing his name on the package. Many foods are simply labeled with a letter *K,* meaning "kosher." Kashrut supervision can vary from semiannual inspection to day-to-day presence in the factory, cannery, or slaughterhouse. When I first went to the supermarket that August five years ago, I was amazed to find a hekhsher on virtually every kind of food in the store.

We should stop talking about kosher food and take a brief field trip to the grocery store. Ready? As we enter we see large stacks of Coca-Cola on sale. Surprise! On every can of Coke is a little K. We walk down the refrigerated aisle and see a K on Philadelphia cream cheese and on Tropicana orange juice. The Vita herring in cream sauce has an O-U. Mrs. Paul's fish sticks, over here in frozen foods, has no sign at all. Either Mrs. Paul lets some seafood without fins and scales into her fish sticks or she's kosher but she's just not letting on. The frozen fried clams—don't even bother looking.

Round the bend and come into the baked goods aisle. Bread presents its own difficulties. Was the pan greased with lard prior to baking, or was lard added to the dough? Look for the hekhsher, because the list of ingredients might not tell the full story. Cereal—here's a K on Total and an O-U trying to look inconspicuous in the lower-right-hand corner of the Puffed Wheat box. Special K, as you might expect, carries a K.

On to crackers. Triscuits now carries the O-U, ever since Nabisco replaced lard with vegetable shortening. (Welcome aboard.) Can Mallomars be far behind? Yes, because they contain gelatin in the marshmallow part. Gelatin is made from animal bone. I wish some Silicon Valley scientists would lay high technology aside for a while and come up with a substitute for gelatin. I miss Mallomars.

No need to worry, though, because we are coming up on the Entenmann's display. Entenmann's now carries the O-U. Next to the hekhsher on some of the products is a capital *D*, which stands for "dairy." This tells you that milk or butter or some other dairy product went into the cake and you therefore cannot serve it after a dinner that included meat. According to Orthodox law, one must not only refrain from eating meat and milk together, and from cooking or serving meat products in pots or dishes used for milk products, but one must wait after eating meat a certain period of time—one, three, five, or six hours, depending on the practice of one's family or group—before one has dairy products again.* Hence the D. Imagine my surprise upon learning of all this *communication* going on between packages of food and observant Jews. When you think about how difficult it must have been to obtain kosher anything if you lived in a European ghetto or a small town in Poland and you compare those times to these, when even peanut butter carries a K, you understand how much easier it is to practice traditional Judaism today. Our great-grandparents would have marveled.

A left turn brings us into the meat aisle. Forget about all the stuff the supermarket itself packages. Not a prayer. The kosher carnivore has three options: leave the supermarket and go to a kosher butcher; buy Hebrew National or 999 salami or bologna; or do what I like to do, buy the ready-to-defrost kosher frozen food available to those, like me, with limited culinary talents.

As long as we are in the meat aisle, we should discuss the idea of "glatt" kosher. Eating nothing but kosher food is symbolic of doing only what is proper in God's eyes. Kashrut imposes discipline—it forces a person to make small choices at all times. If I have a hamburger I cannot have the ice cream afterwards. (Some solve this dilemma by having the ice cream first.) The theory is that confronting small choices regularly makes it easier to make the large ethical choices when life presents them. If one is haphazard about one's kashruth one might be equally sloppy in other matters of Jewish ritual. Since kashruth is important both for its own sake and for the symbolism and discipline it brings to life, some people choose to be even more careful about certain aspects of their observance of kashrut. They will only eat "glatt" kosher meat.

Many people do not know how the term *glatt* evolved. *Glatt* is Yiddish for "flat" or "smooth." When a *shochet*, a ritual slaughterer, kills an animal, he will immediately feel the lung

---

*The idea is to avoid meat and milk mixing even in one's stomach. According to the rabbis, milk and most cheeses pass quickly through the system, so one need wait only after eating meat, which takes longer to break down.

of the animal for bumps. If there are certain bumps or lesions on the lung, the animal died diseased and therefore cannot be considered kosher. Certain other bumps are natural, and an experienced shotchet can tell these various bumps apart. If the lung is flat—glatt, no bumps—then it is perfect, and even the *mehadrin min ha-mehadrin*—the most exacting of Jews—can eat it. If there are certain other, harmless bumps, then the meat is merely kosher, but not glatt.

Glatt kosher itself stirs debate among observant Jews. Some believe that it enhances one's religious practice to be extra careful about the meat one eats, while others find in it aspects of holier-than-thouness. The concept of glatt applies only to cows, by the way. Some butchers nevertheless sell, and some people, out of ignorance, buy, "glatt kosher" chicken, which is like buying "French Wine from Napa Valley" or anything in America with a *le* or *la* in front of it—"La Frozen Dinner," "Le Car." There is no such thing as glatt kosher chicken.

Onward. From meat to condiments. You can find hekh-sherim on a variety of products. Many brands of pickles are fine, as are many kinds of mayonnaise. Mustard (except for mustard made with nonkosher French wine) is fine. Many brands of margarine, horse-radish, and even cooking oil carry some form of hekhsher right on the label.

Let's look at one last product and then we'll hit the checkout counter and go home. Bacos are kosher. Hard to believe, isn't it? Bacos are mock bacon bits, and they carry the O-U. Many Jewish couples who agree on everything else in life argue over whether it is proper to bring home the Bacos. They are perfectly kosher but they look, smell, and taste like the real thing (I've been there—I know), and not every Jewish homemaker wants them in his or her kitchen. If only Bacos were our biggest problem.

Chapter 9

"All Right, What's With the Beanie?"

Sometimes it felt like an umbrella and sometimes it felt like a dime, but I always knew it was there. I was comfortable with every aspect of my experiment with Orthodoxy save one—the yarmulke. It attracted attention in the street, and it confused and frightened my family. I wore it nonetheless in New York that August and during the following school year. It was a lightning rod for conversation and consternation among my relatives and friends. For the first time in my life I heard people on the street say derogatory things about Jews. In Manhattan, a hot dog vendor said something like "Get out of my way, you f——ing Jew." In Holyoke, Massachusetts, twenty minutes from my college town of Amherst, at a minor league ballgame I attended just before the school year began, some local kids told me to "Come here with that little hat, Jewboy." I was fascinated and repelled. It was as though I had put on not a yarmulke but earphones and a radio antenna and now I was attuned to all the anti-Semitic signals in the air that I had never heard before.

The anti-Semitism I encountered only strengthened my resolve to wear the yarmulke. Interestingly, Jewish law does not obligate a person to cover his or her head. Most observant men do so because it is a very strong custom. I suppose the message here for any potential baalei teshuva is make the yarmulke your last step and not your first. It may be best to wait until family and friends have adjusted to other things—your observing the Sabbath or the laws of kashrut—before you wear the yarmulke in public. Of course, this is a decision that every male baal teshuva must make for himself. The outward manifestation of Orthodoxy is much subtler for baalot teshuva—women who become Orthodox. Certain circles in Orthodoxy do not consider it proper for women to wear pants. Many parents of young women who became Orthodox are therefore quite surprised to see their daughters suddenly wearing skirts.

As I said, the greatest stumbling block in the path of observance was my own ignorance. One example will suffice. That August, not long after my return from Israel and Greece, I went to visit my father at an apartment complex to which he had moved since the separation. (This would have been strange enough had religion never entered the picture.) My father and I were grateful, each of us in his own way, for the changes in our own lives that were so difficult for the other to grasp. My father asked me to explain my conversion. Ben Franklin said that it is better to remain silent and be thought a fool than to open one's mouth and remove all doubt. My shallow understanding of Orthodox Judaism must have removed a lot of doubt.

". . . And if the Jews merit it," I said, "then the redemption will come, led by the *mashgiach*," using the Hebrew word for "supervisor of kashrut" instead of the word for "messiah," *mashiach*. I then proceeded to eat cheese of doubtful kashrut on Ritz crackers, which are also not kosher. I then demanded to be taken to a kosher delicatessen, and I would not eat any meat dish because I thought I had to wait six hours after cheese before eating meat. My father may not have gone to yeshiva, but he knew that a supervisor of kashrut would not introduce the millennium, that Orthodox Jews do not eat Jarlsburg cheese on Ritz crackers, and that you wait six hours after meat before you eat milk and not the other way around. He must have wondered how I could be so committed to something I understood so poorly. Family members often asked why I could not explore my spirituality through the Reform or Conservative movement, each of which affords its adherents considerably more flexibility than did Orthodoxy. Looking back, I suppose I was not curious about those branches of Judaism because they seemed to me to lack the ancient authenticity that Orthodoxy claimed. I never succeeded in explaining to my father, or to any of my family, why I was so attracted to Orthodoxy, and I suspect the same is true of the overwhelming majority of baalei teshuva.

The new school year began shortly after that dinner with my father. My friends who knew of the tug-of-war I played with the yeshiva were concerned about me and asked me about the conversion. Everyone else learned quickly that something had happened because I was now covering my head, either with the yarmulke or with a baseball cap, depending on my nerve that day. One nonobservant Jewish friend shook my hand and told me, "I don't know what you're doing, but I'm proud of you."

Religious Christian friends dropped by to ask questions or compare notes, but no one was more concerned than a classmate named Michael Flood. Michael came from Livonia, Michigan, where they don't get too many Jewish people. I met Michael the first week of college in our freshman dormitory. As senior year began, our friendship then three years old, he collared me in the campus snack bar and sat me down. "All right, what's with the beanie," he asked, and he wanted to hear the whole story. We spoke for many hours over the next two evenings. He had two points to make—one, why alienate people who might not understand what the yarmulke meant— why jeopardize my social standing; and two, why do you have to do all these things to be religious? Won't God like you if you are a good person even if you do not keep kosher, and the Sabbath, and everything else?

With his second argument Michael and I had unwittingly stumbled onto the principal sticking points between Judaism and Christianity, and our discussion paralleled those of Jewish and Christian theologians throughout the ages. Although he rarely attended church services, he said, he considered himself a good Catholic because he tried to be a good person and tried to consider the feelings of others whenever he acted. Why was that not good enough for me? Why did I have to do all these things—tefillin, resting and praying on Saturday—and why did I have to let the world know by means of the yarmulke? Wasn't religion supposed to be personal?

I was not entirely convinced that I was right, so I defended my activities on the ground that it was an experiment. As for observing the commandments, I explained, we believe that God entered into a special relationship with the Jews, His Chosen People, not because we were more numerous, or stronger, or simply better than other people. We believe that we were and are none of those things. We cannot explain it, but we believe that God has singled us out for reasons best known to Him, and with that status come responsibilities. For the Jewish people it is not enough to be good and to be moral; we have the blueprint of the universe, the Torah, in our hands, and it is our job to study it and live by its rules. Neither of us convinced the other, although my friend Michael now says that after our conversation I stopped wearing the yarmulke for a few days, something I do not remember.

Amherst is a college of fifteen hundred students. Although Orthodox Jews had attended the college in times past, there were no other yarmulkes on campus during that school year, my last year at the college and my first after the conversion, and I knew of no Orthodox Jews living in the town of Amherst. I did not lack for support, though, thanks to a couple, a rabbi and his wife, who ran a Chabad House on the edge of the University of Massachusetts campus a mile from Amherst College. Most Jewish males in New York City have contact at least once in their lives with the Lubavitch movement, the group that runs campus Chabad Houses across the country, through their "Mitzvah Tanks"—trailers parked on city street corners. The trailers are staffed by young Jews who attempt to cajole passersby into putting on tefillin: "Are you Jewish? Did you put tefillin on today? Did you know Jewish law says you have to put on tefillin?" It is not a pleasant experience. From an early age I associated the Lubavitch movement (and tefillin) with fanaticism and rudeness. I was wary when I first attended the Chabad House, and I had low expectations of the intellectual caliber of the rabbi. I could not have been more mistaken.

To illustrate the rabbi's point of view I should set down a story he liked to tell. It helps to imagine the speaker as a Hasid of twenty-nine years, with a black coat, a homburg, and a bushy beard. It also helps to know that the *Sh'ma*, the line from Deuteronomy that reads in Hebrew *"Sh'ma yisrael, haShem Elokeinu haShem echad"* and in English "Hear, O Israel, the Lord our God, the Lord is One," is the watchword of Judaism, one that a Jew repeats twice every day and in the last possible moment before death, and that *"Baruch shem k'vod malchuto le'olam va'ed*—Blessed is the name of His glorious kingdom forever and ever" is the response, the line that follows the *Sh'ma* in the prayers.

"Two centuries ago, in Poland," Rabbi Yisroel Deren would begin, "the Polish noblemen, fancying themselves Roman dignitaries, would have orgies of food and drink and who knows what else that would last for days. And when the party began to grow dull, the noblemen would send their servants to the local peasant village to find some poor old peasant, and they would bring him up to the master's house, and they would throw him into an arena and force him to wrestle a bear. This was something they believed the Romans used to do, and they found it entertaining.

"At one of these feasts, they sent the servants to the village and they grabbed an elderly Jew, and brought him up the hill to the mansion, and threw him into the arena. He was scared. He had no idea of what to expect. Suddenly someone opened a gate and the bear rushed into the arena. The old Jew cowered with fright and said what all Jews say when they believe the end is at hand—'*Sh'ma yisrael hashem elokeinu hashem echad.*'

"And the bear answered, '*Baruch shem k'vod malchuto le'olam va'ed.*' "

The point, Rabbi Deren would explain, is that in society we all wear masks. Sometimes we wear the mask of a peasant, sometimes that of a nobleman, sometimes that of a college student, sometimes something else. But beneath those masks, when life is stripped away to its most elemental, we are Jews. Chabad House's purpose, he said, was to remove the masks and grasp that fundamental Jewishness. What a coincidence. This was exactly what I wanted to do.

It is fitting that the story was set in eighteenth-century Poland, for it is to that time and place that the Lubavitch movement traces its roots. Hasidism was a movement that grew up at a time when religious Judaism was the exclusive province of those Jews wealthy and intellectual enough to learn in yeshiva. Poor, uneducated Jews found themselves increasingly cut off from their faith until a series of traveling preachers, most notably the one called the Baal Shem Tov, or "Possessor of a Good Name," visited their villages and instilled in them a Judaism of joy, a piety through dancing and delight in the knowledge of God if not in a thorough knowledge of Talmud.

Hasid means "pious one" in Hebrew. The learned world used the term in a derogatory manner to describe the Jews attracted to the movement, as if to call them "pious fools." But the name, and the movement, stuck. Community leaders called rebbes sprang up all over Galicia, the part of Poland where many Jews lived. (It may seem hard to reconcile with Polish-Jewish relations during the Holocaust and the post–World War II anti-Semitism that lives on in Poland long after most of its Jews fled or were killed, but Jews used to believe that Poland was a substitute Promised Land, offering sanctuary to Jews exiled or disgraced in other European countries. To the Jews, "Poland" sounded a lot like *po lin*, ancient Hebrew for "stay here.") Different Hasidic groups took different approaches to Judaism. Chabad considers itself the most intellectual of all the Hasidic sects. Founded by one of the Baal Shem Tov's disciples, Chabad combines the intellectual rigor of the yeshiva with the emotional devotion of the Hasidic movement. They made their headquarters in, and took their name from, the Russian town of Lubavitch, which means "city of love." The group enlarged its numbers under a dynastic series of rabbis and moved to America in 1940 to begin an outreach movement, or perhaps I should say, an "inreach" movement, since they sought to make Jews more religious and not to make non-Jews Jews. This is the same outreach movement that affected me so negatively on the sidewalks of New York. The Lubavitch are not always well-liked because they come into communities and college campuses whether wanted or not. But I admired their nerve and their attitude that there is work to be done and Jews to be educated.

I once asked my mother why the Jews of Eastern Europe did so little when the Nazis came in. It is not an original question, and it still perplexes today. My mother responded that there had always been persecutions and pogroms. They were, sad to say, a regular part of life. The Jews did so little because no one expected the Nazi persecution to be so thorough. At any rate, the Lubavitch had the good sense, or good karma, or both, to quit Eastern Europe and move to Brooklyn, and two of their emissaries, Rabbi Deren and his wife, had made little Amherst, Massachusetts, their base of operations.

The Chabad House provided services and festive meals for Sabbaths and Jewish holidays, as well as dormitory space for four University of Massachusetts students. Those four, along with students from nearby colleges, formed the nucleus of the Chabad community that year. New faces appeared most weeks and were surprised to see the sexes separated during prayer and the noisy, spirited, Lubavitch approach to worship. If they were not scared off by all that, they would join us for dinner.

We sat around long tables and ate large meals and drank vodka and toasted the eighty-year-old Lubavitcher Rebbe, the leader of Chabad.*

Rabbi Deren would *fahrbreng,* or "discuss," Jewish concepts and answer our questions. We were family, the rabbi, his wife, their little children, and the ten or fifteen of us regulars.

---

*Lubavitch Hasidim revere their Rebbe and attempt to instill in everyone they meet admiration for the Rebbe's piety and scholarship.

Together we cooked and cleaned and set the table and conducted services and learned from the Derens about Judaism.
Never during the school year did I think of the Chabad extended family as a substitute for the one that I had lost that
summer, but perhaps that was part of the appeal.

The Derens' role at Amherst was double-faceted—to touch
the lives of as many Jews as they could by means of providing
services, meals, and classes, and, where possible, to convert
one or two Jews a year to the Lubavitch movement itself.
Visitors to the Sabbath dinner table often included Lubavitch
yeshiva students, some of whom were baalei teshuva who had
found their way to observance at the Chabad House of
Amherst, of all places. I also paid several visits to the Lubavitch
headquarters in Crown Heights, deep in Brooklyn, an experience like stepping back in time. There, I passed one Sabbath
with a young surgeon and his wife who had moved from South
Africa to live nearer the Lubavitcher Rebbe so that he could
regularly attend the Rebbe's speeches and religious services. I
asked him as politely as I could whether he was running away
from reality by living in the insular Lubavitch world of Crown
Heights. Part of me feared that I was doing the same thing in
Amherst. He answered without emotion. "Do you consider
eighty hours a week of stitching up gunshot and stabbing
wounds in a Brooklyn hospital running away from reality?"

There was something unreal, nevertheless, about going to
Crown Heights and attending a *fahrbrengen*, or evening of
lectures by the Rebbe himself on Jewish subjects. Several
thousand men would pack themselves into the sanctuary of the
headquarters, a room that could seat comfortably no more than
fifteen hundred. The Rebbe, already in his eighties, would
speak without notes, taking occasional ten-minute breaks,
from nine at night until the early morning. He looked out upon
a sea of black coats and black hats and heavily bearded faces.
Children scampered through legs and under benches. Newcomers like myself found ourselves gently pushed toward the
front so that we could see. Women sat upstairs in a separate
gallery.

The Rebbe spoke in Yiddish, but we could rent small radios to pick up the simultaneous translation offered by a tag team of scholars and broadcast closed-circuit in English, French, Hebrew, and Russian. Whenever the Rebbe stopped, we would stand with small cups of wine in our hands and wait to catch his eye and see him say L'chaim, a toast, directly to each of us. Meanwhile a melody would start from somewhere in the back and thousands of men would sing along. Men and boys would rock on their feet and sing, first softly and slowly, and then, when the Rebbe indicated with a quick gesture of the head that he was listening, the singing would quadruple in volume and intensity, thousands of religious men rocking the rafters of the sanctuary. One sensed that if the Rebbe ever stood up at that moment and said, "Men! Tear down Brooklyn!" Brooklyn would be no more. Of course, he never said anything like that.

The Chabad House at Amherst gave us a small taste of that intensity. I never saw myself as a Lubavitcher, but I was grateful to Chabad for instilling such devotion in Rabbi Deren and his wife as to make them leave home, come to Amherst, and attempt to show us what traditional Judaism was. As a college freshman I had studied a bit of anthropology, and I remember feeling envious toward the tribes we read about, each with its particular customs. Now I had the pleasure of learning about my own people's customs. For example, many observant Jews eat pomegranates on Rosh haShana, the Jewish New Year, because they remind us that even the Jew least connected with observance is as filled with Torah and good deeds as is a pomegranate with seeds. I liked the symbolism because it was our symbolism.

The last of the Jewish holidays in the early fall is Simchat Torah, the Rejoicing in the Law, one of the two days on the Jewish calendar (Purim is the other) when some Jews drink to excess. I arrived at the Chabad House after services had ended. My father was with me—he had come to Amherst to visit. I made Kiddush, the ritual blessing for Sabbaths and holidays, over a full glass of vodka. We danced with the Torah and with each other for hours. My vodka-induced haze was so deep that

I remember little else about the evening. I recall thinking only that Judaism was a wonderful thing and that we had to understand that it should be the central thing in our lives. I tried to communicate these ideas to others present, but the only words I could find were, "We've got to f——k the b——s——s, f——k the b——s——s!" Some Orthodox Jew I was.

Recently I had an interesting conversation with a classmate, a woman I had not seen in the four years since our graduation. I asked her what people thought of my conversion and of its most obvious sign, the yarmulke. She told me that most people who knew me were not convinced that I was wholehearted about Orthodoxy, especially since I kept giving off signs that suggested that the old, irreligious me was alive and kicking. It did not seem like the Michael they all knew.

Looking back, I understand that my friend is right. I did not want to abandon my old self despite my attraction to Orthodoxy. Perhaps if I had done so my transition might have been smoother, but more about that later. Every Wednesday or Thursday of that school year I wondered whether I would observe the coming Sabbath. It was never a certainty until the last minute. And there were Saturday evenings and other nights that I put Orthodoxy out of my mind and returned to earlier social habits. I was doing some things right, though. In addition to Sabbath services, I was attending morning services with two other students; I still refrained from nonkosher meat (I was not ready to cross the border into strict observance of kashrut); and I was learning Torah all the time. The learning came from books I bought on my second visit to the yeshiva and others that I borrowed from the Chabad House. As the fall semester ended, I realized that no one had ostracized me for my Orthodoxy. My friends and professors mostly kept their curiosity to themselves.

During winter vacation, Amherst cosponsored a three-week trip to Kiev, Leningrad, and Moscow, and I went along. It is not hard for American Jews traveling in the Soviet Union to meet Russian Jews. The Soviets often interrogate and treat harshly Russians who make contact with visiting foreigners, but Jews who have applied for exit visas, forfeiting their jobs in the process as a matter of course, have little to lose. I knew that thousands of nonobservant Jewish people had become baalei teshuva like myself. I now learned that baalei teshuva existed even in Moscow.

Fear of losing their jobs forces Russian baalei teshuva to practice their Judaism in secret. They gather in small groups across Moscow, teach each other Hebrew and Talmud, buy meat from an underground kosher shochet, and even ferment their own kosher apricot wine, since grapes are not available in the winter. These Jews live in fear of a government that would prefer to let Judaism die out with the current generation of old people. There is one working synagogue in Leningrad and there are two in Moscow, but I saw few young people attending services in any of them. Economic pressure is not the only trouble facing the baalei teshuva of Moscow. Few of the young Jews' parents are religious. To most of them, Judaism is nothing more than an excuse for oppression by the government. One twenty-five-year-old told me that he did not dare tell his parents that he had begun to study Hebrew until nine months had gone by. They were furious. Why was he doing this to himself? Were things not hard enough already?

The obstacles they faced nevertheless melted away every Friday evening as darkness descended over Moscow and the Sabbath candles filled their small rooms with light. Twice I attended Friday night services and Sabbath dinner with a group of nine Muscovite baalei teshuva. The services they conducted were virtually identical to those I remembered from the yeshiva and to those I attended at Amherst. These young Jews were warm and friendly. Their religion was, perhaps, also their form of protest against the Soviet system. Although I did not know exactly what was motivating me, we expressed in identical manner a need for spirituality inside each of us. When we rose to leave, two of the Russians accompanied us into the street despite the freezing weather. Jewish custom requires accompanying a guest on the first steps of a journey (maybe that is why Jewish goodbyes even today take so long).

"Did you see that," asked one of the other guests, as we walked back to our hotel. "He took his key and tied it to his belt so that he wouldn't have to carry it [and thereby violate the biblical injunction against carrying from inside to outside during the Sabbath]. They try so hard to do it right, it could make you cry."

I do not remember crying, but the experience certainly strengthened my resolve. The Russian trip affected me not only because of the Jews I met there but also because my father's family had emigrated from Russia ninety years earlier. The brief, two-minute service at the conclusion of the Sabbath is called *Havdalah*, or "separation" of the sacred—the Sabbath day—from the beginning of the new week. I remember my makeshift *Havdalah* in Moscow—a can of Russian beer instead of kosher wine, a sweet-smelling orange in place of spices, and a couple of long-necked hotel matches for a braided candle. As my roommate and I doused the matches in the beer, signifying the Sabbath's end, I realized that this was the first *Havdalah* a member of my family had made in Russia in ninety years. Again that feeling of continuity, of connection with generations I never knew, flooded me.

The Jews I met in Moscow could make Orthodoxy work for themselves, despite their precarious position in the Soviet Union. (Best joke I heard in Russia: "What's the tallest building in Moscow?" "KGB Headquarters, because you can see Siberia from the basement.") Surely, I could make the same effort in my safe little college town. My family and friends never saw the yeshiva that had originally brought me close to traditional Judaism; never sat among the yeshiva students sitting in pairs and unlocking the mysteries of the L-shaped blocks of Talmud text; never found themselves moved by the "Structures" rabbi's persuasive cadences. So far, I knew, I had failed to describe adequately what I had seen there that made me take on the yarmulke, the Sabbath, and the other trappings of Orthodoxy. I went back to America aware that I would not be able to explain what I saw in Russia—the baal teshuva community of Moscow, the resolve of whose members to live by Jewish law had strengthened my resolve to do likewise.

Chapter 10

"Are You Still Doing Religion?"

Back in Amherst for the spring term, seven months after the Twelve Days, I was no more convinced that Orthodoxy was correct for me than before I left, but I was certain that I wanted to keep trying. As the weekends approached, whether I would keep the Sabbath became less of a question. Some conflicts did not disappear, of course. Passover was coming. Now that I was observant, I could not eat in my mother's home, or travel to where my father lived after the first night to spend the second night of the holiday with him. This is an opportune moment to explain how I understood the Sabbath and the holidays and why they had affected my planning so quickly.

The Bible says, "Remember the seventh day and make it holy." It amplifies—"In six days you shall work and do all your labor, and the seventh day shall be a day of rest to your God." The question is, how do you make a day of rest "holy"? What does it mean to have a day of rest "to" God? What should you refrain from doing, and what do you do instead? The Bible and the Oral Law, of which the Talmud is the compendium, offer answers. Scholars interpret these words from Genesis to mean that creative work should be avoided on the seventh day; that the Sabbath should be a day of reviewing what there is and not of going out and creating more. Many people know that observant Jews stay home from work on the Sabbath, but fewer people know that the Orthodox also will not ride in a car, turn on a light switch, go to the movies, write letters, or do other things. The reasons for these rules are less well known.

The explanation is found toward the end of the Book of Exodus. By that point in biblical history, the Jews had fled from Egypt, camped in the desert, heard the Ten Commandments at Mount Sinai, and according to one opinion, built the golden calf and worshiped it, fearing that Moses was dead and that God had deserted them in the wilderness. Most of the last third of Exodus is filled with a description of how to build a portable sanctuary that would travel with the Jews as they wandered in the desert. The instructions specify the type of wood for the beams, how they were to be lettered so they could be assembled quickly at the next campsite, how to decorate the sanctuary, how to build the altars inside, how to make the curtains, and so on.

According to one scholar's opinion, this sanctuary standing in the middle of the camp would remind the entire Jewish people that God was watching over them. Six days a week, the entire Jewish people pitched in to build the sanctuary, we read in Exodus, and on the seventh day they rested. Jewish biblical scholars therefore concluded that just as the Jews of the desert spent their working days attempting to create a physical and spiritual reminder of God's existence—the portable sanctuary—so modern Jews should spend their working days attempting the same thing—a portable sanctuary in their hearts.

This, it seemed to me, was the message of Orthodox Judaism. When the Bible says "In six days shall you work," it does not mean, "Go forth, My children, and make a lot of money." It means that one should work at bringing Godliness into the world. Jews are supposed to do this not only by being decent, moral people at home and on the job but also by observing the rest of the commandments—the laws of kashrut, of prayer, of not speaking *lashon hara* (slander), and so on. When the Sabbath comes, we stop building that portable sanctuary in our hearts and we turn around instead and look at what we, as God's partners, have created, and we rest.

Rabbinical scholars long ago concluded that anything the Jews did to build the portable sanctuary in Exodus is something we do not do today on the Sabbath. In the desert they inscribed the beams for ease of assembly; we do not write on the Sabbath. They sewed and dyed material for curtains; we do no sewing or painting or anything similar on the Sabbath. They needed fire in order to work metal into altars and candelabras; a special Biblical prohibition forbade kindling a fire on the Sabbath. We do not make fires or even create sparks, which come into existence every time one flicks on a light switch or starts an automobile ignition or lights up a cigarette. This is why observant Jews will not drive or ride on the Sabbath, or turn on or off any electrical device, or even smoke.

I learned, in my last year at Amherst, that the idea of the Sabbath kept in accordance with Jewish law could still make sense despite all the changes in life since the time of the Exodus. Nothing is as restful; nothing else I knew could let a person attain that mountaintop silence. The laws for the major holidays, such as Rosh haShana (the Jewish New Year) and Passover are similar in most respects to those governing the Sabbath. Since I wanted to adhere to Jewish law, I could not travel on the holiday to split it between my parents' homes.

In the dead of New England winter the sun sets around half past four, and the Sabbath, of course, begins equally early. I was now planning my work week around its arrival, so that when the Sabbath came to Amherst I would be ready. I now realized how difficult it was for observant Jews who worked from nine to five. They had to leave on Fridays as early as two or three, a potential source of conflict between employers and Orthodox employees. Many observant Jews therefore choose jobs that let them enjoy the Sabbath in peace—some work for Orthodox employers; others are self-employed or work out arrangements with their bosses.

I wondered how the Derens could stand it in Amherst. At Lubavitch headquarters in Crown Heights, Sabbath meant thousands of people packing into the synagogue at 770 Eastern Parkway, the Brooklyn sanctuary where the Rebbe's *fahrbrengens* took place, and it meant other observant Jews nearby, people with whom one could visit and study Torah. In Amherst they were isolated. They had only each other and their young children. Rabbi Deren frequently recharged his batteries by traveling to New York. Often that spring I did likewise.

New York last August had been a city of closed doors. All I saw were restaurants I could not revisit, all because chance or fate or *hashgachah pratit*—concern for the small details—had brought me to Israel earlier that summer. But now I learned of kosher restaurants, Orthodox synagogues, and Jewish book stores scattered across Manhattan. The city I thought I knew intimately existed on a different plane for observant Jews, and now I was learning what New York offered them.

Bernstein's on Essex Street is an anomalous restaurant. They serve kosher Chinese food. It was the first kosher restaurant I had visited since that dinner with my father in August. At Amherst my head was the only one covered with a yarmulke, and uneasy lay that head. On a Saturday night in midwinter, Bernstein's is packed with yarmulkes. My people! Imagine my delight. Here yarmulkes were normal. I could have kissed everyone in the restaurant. I had kosher hot-and-sour soup and kosher spare ribs (from a cow—the real thing, of course, was off-limits) and "Pho-nee shrimp," which might have fooled some people but not me. I knew I could have had the same meal for half the money at Wo Hop on Mott Street, but it did not matter. I was home.

Dinner at Bernstein's was especially satisfying because of an experience in midtown Manhattan the night before, Friday night. At the time I did not realize that Friday night services in February took place promptly at sunset, at around 4:30. I was staying at my mother's apartment on the East Side and had walked to the Fifth Avenue Synagogue, an Orthodox congregation on 62nd Street, at half past five. Everyone was leaving. I had missed the entire service.

Temple Emanu-el, the world's largest Reform congregation, was only a few blocks away on Fifth Avenue, so I went there instead. This was my first time in a Reform temple—part of the movement in which I had grown up—since my twin sisters' Bat Mitzvah seven years before. From the outside, Temple Emanu-

el resembles a cathedral, right down to the signboard display-
ing times of services. I arrived for the last fifteen minutes of the
service. Even though I had never been inside, I was familiar
with its order of prayers because I used to hear them broadcast
over the radio when I was seventeen years old and driving to a
part-time job.

Inside, the temple reminded me of all the European cathe-
drals that I had ever visited. The organ played softly and I
could almost smell incense burning. The rabbi wore long black
robes and went bareheaded, as did many men in the congregation. Men and women sat together in what looked more like
church pews than anything I had seen in a synagogue. Loud-
speakers amplified the rabbi's voice. The service was mostly in
English and had none of the life of services in yeshiva or at the
Chabad House.

The whole thing seemed like a Christianized Judaism, a
Judaism sapped of Jewish content. I was struck by how uncomfortable I had become with a service I remembered from my
family's Reform temple in Roslyn. Now that I knew the traditional order of Friday night prayers as practiced by observant
Jews all over the world, now that I knew that an organ at
Jewish services and black robes and bareheaded rabbis were
imitations of Christian services, I could not hold back the tears.

I might not stay Orthodox but I could never go back to
Reform, I thought. After the service, congregants surprised me
by taking out cigarettes and lighting them, smoking directly in
front of the temple on the Sabbath, and then hailing taxis! (I
should not have been so shocked. Reform Judaism, of course,
does not accept Orthodoxy's ideas about riding or smoking on
the Sabbath. I found most remarkable the depth of my negative
reaction to a form of Judaism which only months earlier still
claimed me as a member.) In tears and confusion I stood in the
square across from the Plaza Hotel, and prayed from memory
as much as I could remember of the traditional service.

Another frightening moment came that spring at college.
The religion department had invited a prominent biblical
scholar to speak. I attended the lecture, fearing that his critical

approach to the Bible would poke holes in the Orthodox understanding of Scripture and tumble my spiritual house of cards. A word is in order here about the various theories for the origin of the Bible. In the nineteenth century a group of scholars led by Julius Wellhausen concluded that the Bible was a blend of material from several different sources. This idea of multiple sources is, of course, anathema to Orthodox Judaism; according to Jewish tradition, God dictated the entire written Torah—Genesis through Deuteronomy—to Moses, who wrote it all down.

What did I believe about the Bible's origin? In truth, I did not know what to believe then, and am no more certain today. Robert Block, an Orthodox rabbi in New York, has pointed out that Jews for several thousand years have believed that the Bible is holy and deserves special treatment. A fundamentalist belief in this miracle or that catastrophe as described in its pages is not a prerequisite for being counted as an Orthodox Jew. The critical thing is behavior—whether one acts in accordance with its laws or not.

I sat quaking in the lecture hall, uncertain of my own beliefs, fearing that this distinguished scholar would demolish the Bible and point out the inconsistencies that the yeshiva probably tried to hush up. It turned out that I need not have been so nervous. The burden of the lecture was that important people in Genesis and Exodus came in pairs. Moses and Aaron, Jacob and Esau, Cain and Abel. That was his entire thesis, and was hardly worth the hour we had all invested in it. There is, of course, much more to critical Biblical scholarship than this obvious point. Many non-Orthodox Jews take it for granted, though, that Wellhausen, Freud and others who have written critically of the Bible are absolutely correct. I was not convinced.

Not long afterwards, I discussed the lecture with a professor at Amherst who was something of a mentor to me. He mentioned that he had done a lot of searching himself as to the right way to live, and he had found no guiding principles—not in literature, not in philosophy, and not in his religion. That offhand remark lived with me for quite some time. It suggested two possibilities. Either there are no guiding principles out there, and the whole world is a step away from chaos or perhaps traditional Judaism, its Torah and its Talmud, offer a key—something my professor, himself not Jewish, could not have supposed.

After graduation I took a job in Manhattan and learned a bit more about Jewish life in New York. I attended services at an Orthodox synagogue a few blocks from my mother's apartment. Upon my first visit, the men present asked me whether I was there to say *Kaddish* for someone. *Kaddish* is the Jewish prayer in memory of a relative who has died, a prayer that mentions neither God's name nor death and mourning. Composed in Aramaic, it speaks about the greatness of God and about our desire for peace. A person is required to say *Kaddish* at services three times daily for eleven months after the death of a parent, and then every year thereafter on the anniversary in the Jewish calendar of the death. This is called *yohrzeit*, from the Yiddish words for "year" and "time."

Did I have yohrzeit, the men asked—was today the anniversary of the death of a relative? I was surprised by the question and touched by their concern and of course said no. Later I learned that this minyan, like many in New York and elsewhere, was composed mostly of people there to say *Kaddish*. There were three or four regulars in their thirties or forties, but eveyone else was of retirement age. There were no other people in their teens or twenties. The unhappy conclusion I drew was that in many synagogues—even in some Orthodox congregations—young people show up only when a relative has died.

Another synagogue that rapidly became an important part of my life was not in Manhattan or even in Brooklyn but in what used to be the Fireman's Bar in the suburb of Roslyn, New York, the town where I grew up. The rabbi and his wife, Robert and Beile Block, ran an outpost of Orthodoxy not unlike the Chabad House in Amherst. Few Orthodox Jews live in Roslyn. The rabbi had come to the community five years before, fresh from rabbinical school, at the invitation of a few families who had left the Conservative temple in Roslyn because they wanted something a bit more traditional. Rabbi Block combined Orthodox practice, a thorough understanding of Talmud and of his specialty, Jewish philosophy, and boundless enthusiasm along with a sensitivity about people that seemed almost out of place in one so young. (My mother would say, "He has such an old head.")

I was not the only one drawn to the Roslyn Synagogue at that time. In Iran, the newly empowered Ayatollah Khomeini's policy of killing Jews and confiscating their property caused a massive migration to the West. Several extended families of Iranian Jews settled in Roslyn. Many of them found the Roslyn Synagogue more to their liking than either of the more established Conservative or Reform temples in town. During the week I was getting to know the older men of the East Side Synagogue, Jews whose Eastern European roots were similar to mine. On the weekends I went to Roslyn and learned how much I had in common with the Jews of Iran.

Life in New York was frustrating nevertheless. I longed for the intellectual and spiritual life of the yeshiva in Israel, the bitter taste of the previous August all but forgotten. About this time I began to think seriously of aliyah, which is the Hebrew term for emigrating to Israel. The literal translation of *aliyah* is "going up," in the belief that the land of Israel, the Holy Land, occupies a higher spiritual plane than the rest of the world. People who leave Israel, conversely, are called *yordim*, "the ones who descend," from *yeridah*, which means, "going down." Israel may occupy high ground in a spiritual sense, but it can be a difficult place to live, with its lengthy and compulsory military service, high inflation, and high taxes. Large emigre communities have developed in New York, Chicago, Los Angeles, and other places. If you ask these Israelis whether they intend to return home, they will all say yes. A cousin of mine who lives in Jerusalem offers another explanation for the large number of Israeli expatriates. For two thousand years, she says, it has been in the nature of Jewish people to wander, sometimes of their own choice and sometimes not. Just because the State of Israel has been founded does not mean that this historical predisposition to movement disappears. Our inertia keeps us traveling.

If you are a religiously minded Jew, then aliyah is at least a question, a possibility, if nothing more. Religious Jews take seriously the idea that the land of Israel possesses greater spiritual strength than any other place on the globe. The Talmud suggests that all the mitzvot (commandments, good deeds) that one accomplishes outside Israel are merely preparation for living in Israel; that one should be prepared to sacrifice everything to live in Israel; and that Jewish people, even observant Jews, who live outside Israel are considered (by whom? by God? by other Jews? The Talmud is not clear) as if they worshipped idols. In talmudic terms there are only two regions on the planet: *aretz*—the land of Israel, and *chutz la-aretz*—everywhere else.

For centuries, I was learning, pious Jews have taken these words seriously and have braved dangerous voyages, inhospitable climates, and unwelcoming Turkish, British, or Arab rulers, to live their lives or at least their last days in the Holy Land. Sometimes poverty and anti-Jewish behavior at home spurred them; sometimes they gave up comfort and security to live in Israel. The flurries of emigration from America after the founding of the State of Israel in 1948 and the Six-Day War in 1967 have died down. Most *olim*—immigrants—today are Orthodox Jews who believe in the sanctity of the land and are therefore willing to put up with the Israeli economy, bureaucracy, and military service.

Since observant Jews took aliyah seriously, so did I. I welcomed the challenge of making a life in a country where one's presence mattered. Despite the large observant community in Manhattan and its restaurants and book stores and synagogues, there was something scattered about religious life in the city. It seemed grafted on to secular society, out of place, unfocused. One Saturday I met a college acquaintance in Central Park; I was walking back from the synagogue. "Are you still doing religion," he asked. Doing religion? He made it sound like "doing drugs"—just one more mechanism for coping with life.

Well, yes. I was still doing religion. Almost two years after my initial visit to the yeshiva I was still quite serious about being an observant Jew. By now I had fully adopted the laws of kashrut and prayer. As we said, Jewish males are obligated to pray, in groups if possible, three times daily. In the winter, afternoon prayer must take place between 12:30 and sundown, which comes as early as 4:15 p.m. In offices where there is a large observant Jewish contingent, the men will meet daily for the brief, ten-minute service. Word gets out that there is a minyan in a particular suite of a certain building, and observant people from all over the neighborhood will drop in. I frequently attended one such minyan, impressed that all these businessmen and lawyers took time from their working day to pray.

Once, after services concluded, eleven or twelve of us entered the elevator. A woman got in at the next floor and her face registered surprise at the sight of an elevator full of men with beards and yarmulkes or hats.

"Excuse me," she began, "but why do Orthodox Jews always wear hats, even indoors?"

Someone (not I) explained that it was out of deference to God.

"Oh," she said. "I thought it was because you people are always in a hurry."

The woman was not completely wrong. To live as an Orthodox Jew, even in New York, is to lead a complicated life. Food, the Sabbath, and finding a place to pray during the week all take advance planning, and perhaps we always did seem to be in a hurry. Aliyah—moving to Israel—seemed to offer the chance to live out Judaism in a connected manner.

Looking back, I have to ask myself whether I was seeing things clearly. Perhaps I had become overly apocalyptic. "Certain things in the air here in America disturb me," I wrote then in my diary. "I think about my skeletal knowledge of Germany in the 20's, Russia before the pogroms, Poland before the Second World War. I take stock phrases that describe Jews living here and replace 'United States' with 'Germany' or 'Poland.' For example: 'We Jews have never been as free as here in (Poland).' 'I know that I'm Jewish, but I'm equally proud of my (German) heritage.' 'I want my kids to be brought up like the other (German) kids.'

"There is nothing on the political scene that points directly to coming persecutions. No definite clouds on the horizon. What I see today is blindness to history—a sense that persecution is over for good, that America is the promised land—a sense that Polish Jews had, I know, and that German Jews prospering in the 19th century and up to the 1930's must have had. This complacency scares me more than the swastikas that I see around Manhattan. Israel seems to me to be a place where complacency cannot exist." Shortly thereafter I quit my job, withdrew my savings, and returned to Israel.

Chapter 11

Learning How to Learn

Almost two years had passed between the Twelve Days—my initial visit to yeshiva—and my return to Israel to study. My first order of business was to choose a school. Israel offers the newcomer to Orthodoxy many different types of yeshivot, each as idiosyncratic as its founders. Some emphasize Zionism, others stress Hasidism, and still others lean toward Mussar, an approach concerned with ethical behavior. A few yeshivot permit men and women to study together. Something for everybody. The best way to choose one is to visit many.

When I arrived at Tel Aviv I went straight up the Mediterranean coast to visit a woman I knew who was staying in a kibbutz in the Galilee, near the ancient and mystical town of Safed. We went sightseeing in the northern part of the country and then traveled to Jerusalem together. I was quite moved by the sight of proud Israeli soldiers in their simple uniforms. I was never much of a militarist growing up. Had Vietnam lasted longer I probably would have landed in Sweden. I even had mixed feelings as a five-year-old when Neil Yelsey, my best friend, gave me a G.I. Joe doll for my birthday. Nevertheless, seeing those young men standing tall in the uniform of their own country, speaking as a living language the language that had seemed locked inside those L-shaped blocks of Talmud text, and to think about how their fathers or grandfathers must have suffered in Eastern Europe or Russia or Arab countries was to feel an intense, unforgettable pride in that little country. I will also never forget the face of the hotel owner in Jerusalem when I checked in with Janet, who was quite beautiful, and we asked for separate rooms. (I was Orthodox, and this was Israel.)

After Janet left, I visited a yeshiva at Beit El, a new settlement on a hilltop in Shomron, north of Jerusalem, on the West Bank. The students of the yeshiva and the families of the little town lived then in simple prefabricated houses. At the center of the settlement stood an architectural masterpiece. The synagogue and beit midrash seemed to be constructed entirely of glass. As one sat to learn or pray, one could see the rough, rocky hills stretching for miles into the distance.

At the yeshiva I met some baalei teshuva from America and was much impressed by their courage to live here. I also felt a little less alone—here were other people who had taken the large step and had become observant themselves. At that time, the Beit El yeshiva did not have a program for beginners, which meant that I would have to look elsewhere. As the bus bumped back to Jerusalem, the late winter sun darting among the hills, the radio played John Lennon's "Imagine." As often happens on long-distance bus trips in Israel, the driver and many of the passengers quietly sang along.

The next day in Jerusalem I visited four or five other yeshivot and finally settled on one, Yeshivat ha-Mivtar, better known as Brovender's, named for its founder and leader. The atmosphere in the small, slightly shabby beit midrash appealed to me. It turned out to be a good choice. I had come to yeshiva to solidify my practice and understanding of observant Judaism, to learn how to study the original sources for myself—the Talmud, the Chumash, and the various codes of Jewish law, to determine whether I should seek rabbinical ordination and to decide whether I thought it best to live in Israel. Brovender's seemed to offer what I needed.

To picture Brovender's, imagine a graduate school with neither examinations nor grades, where everyone from the dean down to the least-lettered student studies together in the same room, out loud, where the professors have no offices and no privacy, in a quiet neighborhood on the edge of a war zone.

The paint was peeling off the walls and the floor could have stood a good washing, quite a contrast to the elegant, subdued, spotless beit midrash at Ohr Samayach. The dormitory was even worse. The faculty, however, followed the lead of Rabbi Brovender and taught in a relaxed, offhand manner. There seemed to be none of the coercion on the part of teachers or other students. At Brovender's I would not hear the broken record I heard at Ohr Samayach: "Why go to Greece? Your people needs you here!"

Learning Talmud did not come easily for me. The "Brovender's method" was to give newcomers to Talmud study the literal translation of a dozen lines of Talmud text and then have us sit in pairs all morning and figure out the meaning. (This is not as easy as it sounds.) The next morning's class would be devoted to explaining and understanding yesterday's chunk of text, and then the teacher would give us ten or twelve new lines. Afternoon classes in Bible and Jewish law worked the same way. In the evenings were two classes to choose from, one on the Prophets (the section of the Bible after the Five Books of Moses) and another on the Midrash, a collection of rabbinical flights of fancy and offbeat scriptural interpretations.

Like many baalei teshuva, I found it difficult to absorb new material every day in two foreign languages—Hebrew and Aramaic—in an alien mode of syntax and expression, in a place where I knew no one. I was watchful for signs of coercion and fearful of getting swept up in something I did not fully understand. The beit midrash—the study hall—was noisy and crowded. Students and teachers paced and banged their desks or hollered for emphasis (and perhaps, a tiny bit, for show). At Brovender's, as at most yeshivot, there were few diversions—no student newspaper, no glee club, no athletics to loosen the tensions. Morning after morning, I was stretched to the limits of my intellectual competence and emotional strength. We learned for hours at a time—often for ten or twelve hours a day. At night, in my cramped, unheated dormitory room, lying on the thin board and two-inch-thick foam-rubber mattress that passed for a bed, I wondered what I was doing to myself, whether I was perhaps punishing myself for having had it too easy back home. And yet I was learning Torah. I was making those L-shaped blocks my own. I was giving myself the tools to learn more of them after I left yeshiva, to continue to unlock the mysteries of my people's ancient knowledge. I was lonely, and my emotions shot up and down almost daily, but I was making progress. I was acquiring Torah, or at least trying to do so.

"What excites me most about the whole Jerusalem business," I had written a friend almost two years before, while I was still in Greece after the initial twelve days, "What excites me most is that the most brilliant, penetrating minds of the last three or four thousand years have found satisfaction in the study of Torah and after only a few hours I caught a glimpse of what it was that offered them that satisfaction." Now I was becoming one of "them." Whenever I looked up from my text to see a newcomer standing in the doorway of the beit midrash, the central study hall, I had to smile. I remembered the feeling of looking on in confusion and interest. To the newcomer, though, I was simply part of the scenery, just one more yeshiva student rocking in his chair, rubbing his forehead, playing absent-mindedly with his yarmulke, or animatedly attempting to convince his study partner across the table of the correctness of his interpretation. Learning Talmud meant more than the acquisition of religious knowledge. It was a community activity, a shared intellectual adventure. It meant taking my small place in the chain of Jewish history, staking my claim to my complicated heritage.

To be honest, I was not studying constantly—I was also meeting observant women. Brovender's has a women's branch three blocks away. There is only one pay telephone for both schools. The Israeli economy has been on a war footing since before the state was founded, and there are probably more working pay telephones in Kennedy Airport than in all of Jerusalem. Installing and repairing telephones is a luxury that the battered Israeli economy cannot always provide. Even telephone books are scarce and out-of-date; years pass between printings, something Americans, who get new telephone books every year, find hard to understand. But no Brovender's student ever complained that the women did not have their own telephone. How else could we have met them?

Between dinner and evening classes I often waited by the telephone, pretending to have to make a call, so as to meet the women students, some of whom were up to the same thing. At Amherst there were few women with any understanding of or interest in Orthodox Judaism and I always had to explain myself. The women at Brovender's not only understood but they felt the same way I did, and some were new to Orthodoxy themselves. When I looked over my diary as preparation for writing about Brovender's, I was hoping to find insights into Torah and quotable remarks about the yeshiva and its students and teachers. No such luck. I wrote mainly about the women I was meeting.

These women taught me that not everyone accepts the idea of *shidduchim*—the arranged dates that Frank had described in the bar my first night at Ohr Samayach. The idea is rather "black hat," or right-wing—favored only by those Jews who wear black hats as part of their religious attire. Interestingly, you can tell a lot about a person in Orthodoxy by the way he covers his head. A black hat is worn by someone on the far right of the observant spectrum, but only by someone who is from America, is Hasidic, or attends a German- or Lithuanian- (Eastern European) style yeshiva. Right-wing Sephardic Jews and sons of families that emigrated from English-speaking countries and who study in Zionistic Israeli yeshivas wear oversize white knitted kippot, with a dark band of color a third of the way in. (*Kippa*, and *kippot* in plural, is the Hebrew equivalent of the Yiddish word *yarmulke*.) Young American Jews, those who generally think of themselves as "modern Orthodox," wear knitted kippot of different colors—orange or green or blue. These kippot often have the names of the owner embroidered along the side, or perhaps a pattern depicting the walls of the Old City of Jerusalem, or the name of the business they work for ("Lou's Kosher Pizza").

By the way, if a girl knits a boy a yarmulke, she is serious about him and is trying to let him know it. More religiously inclined modern Orthodox young men will wear black knitted kippot, a halfway point between yarmulkes and hats. Young Israelis who cover their heads because their parents insist on it sport kippot the size of silver dollars. Americans are more likely than anyone else to wear kippot that match the color of their clothing. The trained observer can take one glance at a kippah and divine where the wearer goes to yeshiva, where he came from, how he feels about Zionism, and the extent to which he would trust the kashrut of your house.

People who wear yarmulkes which send off signals about religion, background, and attitude are stereotyping themselves. I was amused at first and then saddened by the hidden language of yarmulkes, which are not supposed to be spiritual billboards. They should indicate only one thing—reverence for God. The variety of styles is a divisive force in Judaism, pointing out the differences between Jews rather than accentuating all that we have in common.

I also met women who had grown up in Orthodox homes and who were more comfortable with shidduch dates and rabbinical imprimaturs than with chance encounters at pay telephones or on long bus rides, which is another method for meeting people in Israel. Since we are speaking of dating, a word is in order about sex and Orthodoxy. Many Orthodox young people refrain from all manner of physical contact with the opposite sex before marriage. Even among those unmarried people who engage in physical contact, premarital sex is not acceptable. The rules were less of a concern fifty or a hundred years ago, when people generally married in their late teens or early twenties. Today, when people often do not know what graduate school they will attend, let alone where they will live or whom they will marry, until their mid-twenties, it is difficult to go all those years without some expression of one's sexuality. I suppose more goes on between some unmarried Orthodox couples than did two or three generations ago. But a lot less goes on than in the secular world I knew.

We should tackle a few misconceptions that some people hold concerning sex and Orthodoxy. First, Orthodox men and women do not make love through a sheet. Strange to report, many people believe this. More than a few people worked up the nerve to ask me if I really intended to make love to my wife through a sheet. I do not know where this idea came from. Second, Orthodox women do not have to shave their heads when they get married. A tiny fraction of Hasidic women do so, but that is a custom pertaining to a small group. No Orthodox woman I ever met shaved her head.

Finally, Orthodox Judaism—at least its left wing—does permit the practice of birth control by methods other than rhythm and abstention. Surprised? I was. As for abortion, it is universally permitted in order to save the life of the woman carrying the fetus, and in more lenient circles it is permissible in other circumstances as well. Orthodox couples do not make love during the time surrounding menstruation, but this has nothing to do with "uncleanliness." It has to do with a complicated notion of ritual purity. Many nonobservant friends of mine had heard about refraining from sex during the period surrounding menstruation and asked me why I would involve myself with a group that held women to be "dirty" during an event which is a natural part of life. I explained as best I could that "dirty" is not the thought behind the rule, but I lacked the knowledge then to explain exactly why. Enough myths shattered for now. Back to our story.

Whenever I think about yeshiva students learning Torah for ten or twelve hours a day for months and years at a stretch, I marvel at their concentration. I found studying Talmud intellectually difficult and physically and emotionally exhausting. Four months after my arrival, a full two years after the Twelve Days, I had dropped twenty-five pounds and had not an ounce of energy left. Why was it so hard for me?

The Talmud is written in a combination of Hebrew and Aramaic, the language people spoke in the Middle East eighteen hundred years ago. There is no punctuation. There are few paragraph breaks. The thought process is different from anything I had known until then—ideas slowly built one on top of the other, comprehensible only through references to lines from Scripture or from somewhere else in the Talmud, each of which has to be looked up and understood in context. The legal concepts were foreign to me. Many of the religious concepts were also new to me and hard to accept, especially the distinctions in religious practice between men and women. And I could never forget that my very presence in yeshiva, in Israel, was disturbing to my family, made them feel guilty, made them believe that I had lost control of myself. Whenever I remembered that friends and family thought my newfound religious expression was merely the result of overreaction to my parents' divorce, or "brainwashing," or both, my concentration would vanish.

"I believe what people have been saying about me," I wrote in my diary at one such low moment, "that I adopted Orthodoxy as a reaction to my parents' divorce. What makes me say this? Perhaps because the Orthodoxy I believed in doesn't exist. Or maybe I haven't looked hard enough. Or studied hard enough. Too much faith that faith would eventually come. These are hard words to write. I feel a bit burnt out. Coming closer to the God of Abraham has not lost its charm. What has?"

By "the Orthodoxy I believed in" I meant a sort of fantasy-religion world, a place where people somehow could rise above all the faults attendant to being human, a place where people thought of nothing but God and Judaism and each other's feelings all day long. This may sound like heresy, but learning what was inside the Talmud was also something of a disappointment. The Talmud, completed over a thousand years ago, is an enormous compendium of Jewish law, history, and opinion. Ever since the day my Sunday school librarian had showed us those mysterious L-shaped blocks of text, I had assumed that their study would reveal why Judaism's understanding of God and the universe was the correct one. Instead, at yeshiva I was studying the Talmud and learning how Jews interpreted various biblical verses, how they lived in ancient times, how they worshiped and how they strayed. I had expected the Talmud to explain *why* I should believe in God and Judaism; instead, I was only learning *how* to do so. Faith, I concluded, as did generations of yeshiva students before me, would have to come from within.

Most of the yeshiva students were Americans and South Africans, but I managed to meet some Israelis my age outside the school. Compulsory military service for Israeli males currently lasts three years and begins at age eighteen. So as not to lose the thread of their Talmud studies, many observant young men stretch out their military service, spending three months in uniform and two in yeshiva, shuttling back and forth for a full five years. Their military units are considered to be among the finest in the Israeli Army. Their Zionistic slant on Torah study combined with a religiously inspired love of country makes them equally resolute in battle and beit midrash.

One of my Israeli friends, Amos, was a hesdernik, as religious soldiers on the five-year plan are called, and I often spent Sabbath meals with him. I learned how the hesder soldiers' parents generally delighted in their sons' Zionism and Torah study. I remember in particular one Sabbath we spent in Netanya, a seacoast town north of Tel Aviv. We sat late that Saturday afternoon on the landscaped promenade overlooking the Mediterranean, Amos and his friends comparing notes about tanks, cannons, submachine guns, and rabbis they shared in yeshiva. I am hardly the first to experience or to describe the stark contrast between the peacefulness of a Sabbath, or even a weekday, in the countryside of Israel and the tokens of war that were everywhere, but the casual talk about teachers and tanks, classes and cannonfire jumbled together was hard to put out of my mind.

The hesder soldiers generally had the encouragement of their families, something, of course, that I did not enjoy. Like Amos, some had emigrated to Israel with their families while they were still in their teens. None of those parents, of course, wanted to see anything happen to their children in uniform, but it was a risk that they and their sons had chosen to bear for the greater good of the Jewish people. (When I went to discuss the mechanics of aliyah—moving to Israel—at an organization for Western immigrants, I was told that married men served less time than unmarried men, and married men under twenty-nine with a child served the least of all newcomers. "This is what we in Israel call planned parenthood," the counselor smiled.)

Although I did not envy Amos and his friends their combat duty, especially when a war in the north seemed imminent, I envied the support they enjoyed of their families and friends. Their Zionism, Judaism, and army service all blended together into a cohesive whole, the sort of wholeness that I could not find in New York. I still felt alone, fragmented, cut off from friends and family, and I had the nagging feeling that the Orthodox world into which I was trying to assimilate was not entirely welcoming of baalei teshuva. More about this last point later.

My Hebrew and Aramaic vocabulary slowly increased, as did my ability to translate and understand talmudic argument. My role model was Danny, the hero of Chaim Potok's *The Chosen,* the boy who held his Talmud class rapt as he deftly juggled ideas and explanations and commentaries. I awoke before six each day to attend an early-morning prayer service, reviewed my lessons on the bus to the yeshiva (I had taken an apartment in Jerusalem so as to escape the all-embracing nature of yeshiva life), studied almost without a break, all day long, and was in bed by ten o'clock so as to be ready for the next morning. But to study so intensely during the day with little emotional or physical relief was to allow the demons to prey at night. By July, two full years after the Twelve Days and after only four months in yeshiva, I was utterly exhausted.

I spent a week with my Netanya friends, reading novels, eating banana pancakes (my hosts made me banana pancakes every morning in an effort to fatten me up a bit), and resting on the beach. I slept late, a luxury unknown to the diligent yeshiva student, every morning except one. On that morning I was awakened at twenty minutes to six by singing and laughing outside my window. They must be picnickers, I thought, on their way to the beach, as I looked out the window and considered the line of happy people bearing trays of food down the street. But who goes on a picnic at twenty to six in the morning? Then I remembered that there would be a Bar Mitzvah ceremony in the synagogue that morning. It would start at six because it was a weekday and everyone had to go to work afterwards.

I dressed, walked the two blocks to the synagogue, put on my tefillin, and joined in the fast-paced morning services. Perhaps twenty-five of us were in attendance. The rabbi moved the Torah scroll from the Ark at the appropriate moment (as someone had done on that first morning at Ohr Samayach when I peeped through the parapet window). The boy whose Bar Mitzvah it was approached with sureness, pronounced the blessings, read his part, and watched his father take two photographs. (The flash did not work the first time.) None of the boys or men present wore suits or ties, which Israelis consider overly formal dress, especially in the summer. All concerned wore cotton shirts and slacks. The boy finished and his family trilled their approval. The service concluded and we went to the lobby for drinks, cake, and congratulations. The family packed up the leftovers and we all departed. Elapsed time: oh, about forty-five minutes.

When I was thirteen my own Bar Mitzvah was a big production which I was too shy to enjoy. *Bar Mitzvah* is Aramaic for "son of the commandment." It signifies that thirteen-year-old boys and (twelve-year-old girls) are adults in the eyes of Jewish law. No celebration is required—coming of age is enough. Extravagant Bar Mitzvahs are the norm in much of American Judaism. Since they are the only contact many young Jews have with their heritage, they assume that Judaism is all show and no substance. The simple ceremony I attended in Netanya, over practically before it started, reminded me that such need not be the case.

The vacation did not cure me—I was still worn out and I could study no longer. "In the morning you will wish it were evening, and in the evening you will wish it were morning," reads a warning from God to the Jewish people in Deuteronomy lest they misbehave on a national scale. I felt as though the verse had been written to describe how I felt just then—that time could not pass fast enough to shake off the unhappiness and fatigue I was feeling.

"Malaise," I wrote in my diary. "I am bored, restless; that sinking feeling again. All right, so I'm not going to be a *talmid chachum* [an expert]. I'd like to be free again, to shake off the yoke." I did not realize it then, but my total-immersion approach was not the best way to enter Orthodoxy. A gradual path might have been better. But at that moment I wanted only one thing—to go home. And so I did.

The rabbi and his wife at the Roslyn Synagogue needed a vacation at that time and asked me to fill in. By that point, two years and two months after the Twelve Days' exposure to Orthodoxy, I knew enough of the service to lead an Orthodox congregation in prayer. I say this not out of pride (although I was quite proud at the time) but to illustrate that as foreign as the Orthodox service might seem at first, anyone can master it in a very short time, make it one's own, and use it as a vehicle for approaching God and tying oneself through it to the Jewish community of the past, present, and future.

A brief word about Jewish prayer. Jewish males are obligated to pray three times a day; Jewish women, at least once daily. The afternoon and evening services each take five or ten minutes. Morning and evening services are easy enough to work into one's schedule—set the alarm to go off earlier for the morning service; make some time around dinner for the evening prayers. The afternoon service, called *mincha,* is the tricky one. Jewish law requires its adherents to *daven mincha,* to "pray the afternoon service," between midday and sunset, when most people are at work or at school. I have prayed that service in my college and law school libraries, in bookstores, on buses and subways, in parks and on the mezzanine level of Shea Stadium—in short, wherever I found myself during the afternoons. The rabbis viewed the afternoon service as symbolic of

Judaism's connectedness with our daily lives—a link between the spiritual and the material. Not long ago I read in the newspaper of a neighborhood coalition in Brooklyn between Hispanics and Orthodox Jews. When asked how it was working, the Hispanic leader jokingly replied, "Everything is fine, but every time there's a long meeting they have to stop to pray." I know how he feels.

The Roslyn congregation was small—about thirty-five—enthusiastic, and forgiving of my mistakes. They were patient as I stumbled through the Torah reading, and yes, I was thinking of how not long before I had stood on that parapet in Jerusalem and watched uncomprehending as yeshiva students read from an identical Torah at their services that Thursday morning. If I forgot the melody for a particular prayer, the congregants were not shy about reminding me. Many of them were newcomers to Orthodoxy themselves, and they were finding their way and enjoying the learning process just as I was. In me, I think, they saw a little bit of themselves.

After a few weeks the rabbi and his wife returned, their synagogue intact—my uncertain performance had scared no one off. The High Holidays approached, and once again I faced the dilemma many baalei teshuva know well—do you spend the holiday with your family, as you should, or do you go to an Orthodox synagogue, as you feel you must? Ironically, one of Orthodoxy's main attractions for baalei teshuva is the closeness of families at holiday times; unfortunately for baalei teshuva, not *their* families.

By late September, two years and three months after the initial Twelve Days' exposure to Orthodoxy, I had to decide what to do with the coming year. I considered teaching Jewish day school or taking some other sort of job, and went on some interviews, but my heart was not in it. I wanted to go back to Jerusalem and give learning one last serious attempt. Why did learning Talmud mean so much to me—why do baalei teshuva place so much emphasis on spending lengthy periods in yeshiva?

Learning Torah on a daily basis, or better yet, a twice-daily basis ("You shall learn . . . at your lying down and at your rising up") is a supreme commandment in Judaism. In *Fiddler on the Roof*, Tevye sings that if he were a rich man, among other things, he would sit and learn Torah all day long. Tevye understood that you are not a part of things in the Orthodox world if you do not continuously learn Talmud and its commentaries. Some people attend a *daf yomi*—a Talmud class that covers two pages a day—early every morning or late every night. I know of one Brooklyn couple that switched apartments just so they could live closer to a daf yomi class. One of the highest compliments you can pay in Orthodox circles is to say that someone has "fixed times for learning"—that he has the discipline and desire to let nothing come between himself and the Torah, and he sits down to study twice daily. In some ways, Judaism *is* sitting and learning Torah. If I were to become a part of the Orthodox community, I reasoned, I had to improve my ability to learn.

I had recovered my strength and my desire; the holiday sealed it for me. Back to Israel. I returned to Brovender's, and this time, everything clicked. Once more I was Odysseus, the man who came back after everyone had given up on seeing him again. I settled into a routine that included time for the occasional solid restaurant meal, a modest social life, and frequent escapes to my cousins' Jerusalem home for a break from all that was holy. When I say a modest social life I mean modest. We did not discuss sex much in the yeshiva or even in the dormitory late at night; the locker room and the beit midrash were a poor mix. But two moments stand out, one my first week back and one during my last month, when I went sightseeing in Eilat, among other places. The first experience was in a Hebrew University dormitory, the same University that had let my friend Steven down two years before. (If he had liked Hebrew U., would I ever have become Orthodox? Hmm.)

Another yeshiva student invited me to his cousin's dormitory suite for dinner. As we began to eat, two of his friends, a young man and woman, emerged from the bedroom. He was tucking his shirt in; she was pulling a long T-shirt down just below her thighs. It was one thing to refrain from sexual involvement, something Orthodoxy asks of its unmarried members; it was another, much more difficult thing to confront vivid reminders that other people—younger people—were getting plenty, even if I was not.

The second experience was in the middle of the night in a hotel room in Eilat. My overnight bag awoke me. I turned the light on to find it dancing on its little shelf, doing a jig with a plastic bottle of mineral water. I wondered whether I was dreaming or whether I had finally lost my mind. Then I realized that the little shelf in my room was the extension of the bedboard next door. My overnight bag and water bottle were keeping time with the couple noisily making love in the adjoining room. I knew well by then that religion entailed sacrifice, but this was beyond sacrifice; this was torture.

In the months between these bursts of sexual frustration I managed to make measurable progress with my learning. By the following March—almost three years after the Twelve Days—I could pick up virtually any Hebrew text and slowly make my way through it, understanding the religious concepts on at least a basic level. That fall, I would begin law school back in the States. By then I could make decisions about my own religious practice based on first-hand contact with the texts and not merely on the interpretations of other people. This was a milestone for me. In less than three years I had come from neophyte to thinking, contributing member of the Orthodox community, or so I thought.

Chapter 12

Strangers and Sojourners

Brace yourself for the surprise ending: I didn't live "happily ever after" as an Orthodox Jew. Baalei teshuva have not one but two hurdles to clear on their paths to traditional Judaism. They must assimilate Orthodox Jewish religion—kashrut, the Sabbath, and the rest—and they must merge with Orthodox Jewish society as well. Orthodox Judaism has its own popular music (a soft rock sound with lyrics about Jerusalem and other traditional Jewish themes), its own syntax (an English flavored with Yiddish and Hebrew expressions), and a strongly developed sense of who belongs and who does not. Some Orthodox Jews look upon newly observant Jews as a revitalizing force. Many more, however, have the same neutral-to-negative feelings about baalei teshuva that secular Jews have about Orthodoxy. The lack of understanding about the Jews across the great spiritual divide, sad to say, is mutual.

Nothing in yeshiva prepared me for the suspicion and lack of acceptance I encountered. I can understand how Jews born Orthodox feel. After all, many Orthodox Jews feel their values threatened by secular society—its divorce and intermarriage rates, its media's emphasis on the physical and the sexual. A baal teshuva, from their point of view, is someone who arrives in the Orthodox camp after a lifetime of cheeseburgers, of working on Saturday, and of socializing on Friday night, who suddenly "gets religion" after doing everything that Orthodox Jews are not supposed to do, and then announces, "Here I am,

Orthodox Jews! I've put all that stuff behind me! Treat me as one of your own!" Of course the Orthodox find themselves in a difficult position.

The Talmud nonetheless states that "a baal teshuva can stand in a place where a completely righteous person cannot stand." Commentaries explain that baalei teshuva—those who have known and rejected a non-Orthodox way of life—are even more commendable than those born Orthodox who never know temptation. Baalei teshuva could do with a bit less commendation in the abstract, and a bit more understanding and warmth in the here-and-now. The Orthodox community itself admits that the problem exists—today, synagogues and religious organizations hold lectures and discussions on "The Baalei Teshuva and Their Acceptance in the Orthodox community." Barriers to acceptance evidence themselves in many forms, from insulting comments ("I've seen you baalei teshuva, and I know for a fact that your commitment never lasts" or "Your Orthodoxy will fade like a suntan") to anxious questions ("Really? You don't come from a kosher home? You went to public school? Your parents don't keep the Sabbath?") to the desire of many parents to steer their children away from marrying baalei teshuva ("After all, the grandchildren couldn't eat in our in-laws' house—it would be too confusing for them").

Over five years I repeatedly encountered all of these attitudes and more. For every Orthodox Jew delighted that an assimilated Jew had "come home" ("Where did you go right," asked one such sympathetic person) there are many more who are indifferent to baalei teshuva, or who dismiss baalei teshuva as temporarily religious, as people who could not handle their responsibilities and had turned to Orthodoxy for relief the way other people turn to drugs or alcohol. Some baalei teshuva do embrace Orthodoxy because their secular lives are falling apart. But the majority of the newly observant Jews that I met in America, in Israel, and in Europe were serious people who loved their Judaism despite their initial lack of understanding of its laws and customs, and who withstood the laughter and anger of their families and friends when they displayed commitment to their people and their past.

Baalei teshuva are often confused by the disparity between the Orthodox community's strict observance of Jewish ritual and its seeming lack of interest in *ahavat yisrael*, the commandment to love one's fellow Jew. The following two examples illustrate this point. If they were the only unpleasant moments during my five years of observance I might still be fully Orthodox. Unfortunately, they were not isolated occurrences.

The first episode took place just before Passover two years ago. I was wandering through Central Park with a friend from college when we came upon an old man with a shopping bag. He called himself the Poet O, and he wandered through the park looking for lovers or others to buy one of his poems, which he kept in a few large shopping bags. He came upon us and asked fifty cents for a poem and a blessing. We gave him fifty cents. He asked us to join pinkies. He was a pleasant, almost silly-looking man in his sixties with a ring of white hair and a bemused expression, and we could not disobey. We stood on a Central Park footpath, pinkies locked, and he called upon heaven and earth to bless us and our friendship and the spring and New York and so on. He sold us a second poem, and sensing a sucker in me, was about to sell us a third when suddenly he turned pensive.

"Passover's coming, and I don't have a place to go for the Seder. I don't have any family—I live in an old-age home in Times Square."

The Poet O thus transformed himself from a carefree street person into a lonely old man. He said that he had not been to a Seder for forty years, but this time he wanted to attend one. Not only that, he wanted to attend a fancy Seder on the East Side. I took his address and promised I would find him a place.

At home the next day I called around and learned, much to my dismay, that the going rate for the Seders—the two evening-long commemorative meals filled with ritual recalling the Jews' exodus from Egypt—was one hundred dollars. But a promise was a promise. I made a reservation in his real name at the East Side synagogue I attended and sent the Poet O a letter at the nursing home. I then realized that all I had done was enrich a caterer by one hundred dollars because the Poet O would never show up.

But he did. As I was leaving the synagogue after services to go to my mother's apartment for the Seder, I saw him coming up the street, his yellow shopping bag full of poems and his ring of white hair illuminated for a moment by a street light. He wore the same sweet smile, and all was well with the world, until a few weeks later, when by chance I met him again in the park.

"How was Passover?" I asked.

"Oh, it was wonderful. I told all of the other people at the home that I met this lovely young man in the park and he was making a reservation for me at the East Side Synagogue and they all said I was crazy, I was dreaming, I didn't meet anybody. But the Seders were so beautiful, and the cantor sang so well, and the roast beef was this thick–" and he held his thumb and forefinger an inch apart. "It was the best meal I had in years, and the Seder reminded me of my grandparents and my childhood. I wrote you a letter to thank you—it's here in my bag–" and he rummaged through his sack of poetry and handed me a letter. The letter began, "May the God of Abraham, Isaac, and Jacob bless you for the kindness you showed the Poet O this season."

He continued. "But they treated me terribly at your synagogue. You should have a word with them. When I arrived they said, 'Get out of here, you're a bum!' But I was insistent, and I said, 'No, one of your members paid for me, look on your list!' And my name was right there, next to yours, and they had to let me in. And when I came to my table the people screamed, 'Oh! He's a bum! He can't sit here! And they insisted that they get moved to another table. So I sat by myself.' "

My first thought was that I could never show myself in that synagogue again—I should have known better than to sponsor a street person at an elegant seder. My second thought was that the Passover Haggadah—the service that accompanies the meal—begins when the leader holds up a piece of matzah, called the *lechem oni*—"bread of affliction" but translated more accurately as "poor man's bread"—and says, "Whoever is hungry, let him come and eat. Whoever is [spiritually] needy, let him take part in our Passover." I was naive enough to think that people actually believed this, but when they were put to the test, when an old man without family or money came to their table, they called him a bum and demanded different seating. This was not what I expected from Orthodox Jews, or from anyone, for that matter.

Imagine my surprise, shortly after Passover, to find an advertisement in the personals column of the *Village Voice* that began, "Modern Orthodox Jewish woman seeks male 21–25" and ended with box number VV-826. I wrote a long, silly letter to the box number about how we would meet and fall in love and get married and spend our honeymoon on the Falkland Islands, then the scene of a war between England and Argentina. A few weeks later the telephone rang. It was the woman from Box VV-826.

We met for lunch. She was pleasant. She and a girlfriend had taken out the ad for a lark and had received eight or nine letters, but mine was the funniest. (Why, thank you.) Over our meal we talked of our different backgrounds. She had been born into an Orthodox Jewish family and was raised on Manhattan's Upper West Side, home of a large observant community. As we paid and stood to leave, she confessed, "I knew you had to be a baal teshuva. A frum guy would never have written a letter to the *Village Voice*."

The Yiddish word *frum* meant two different things to us. I thought it meant "observant"; she seemed to define it as "someone from an observant home."

"Wait a minute. I'm frum," I protested.

"No, I mean frum. You know, a frum guy," she said, dismissing me. Frum, to her, was something I could never attain. Frum had more to do with where you came from than what you believed or how you practiced. Frum was a fact of birth, not of faith. "That's not right," I thought—"I put on tefillin, I keep Sabbath, I keep kosher just like people who grew up observant." If anything, I was more careful about certain aspects of Jewish practice than some Jews who had known of it all their lives. I felt like Charlie the Tuna. "Sorry, Charlie. Only Jews that were born Orthodox can be Star-Kist."

My passage to Orthodoxy can be divided neatly into two periods: The first was the cocoonlike time of the Twelve Days, the trip to Greece, and the Chabad House of Amherst (the first year). The second was the time I spent living among Orthodox Jews (the last four years). During the first period, my contact with the Orthodox was limited to the students I met in yeshiva and to adults whose lifework included working with newly observant Jews. Although I found yeshiva studies difficult (who doesn't?), I never thought seriously of shaking off the yoke of Orthodoxy until I spent time in the "real world" of current-day Orthodox Jewish culture. The two events I outlined just now—the Poet O's Passover and my blind date—are extreme examples of a not-so-subtle phenomenon in the Orthodox world today, namely, a mistrust of outsiders, including baalei teshuva.

I interviewed a number of baalei teshuva as preparation for writing this book. Most of them responded to articles about the book that appeared in various Jewish publications. One woman called me after an article appeared in the *Jewish Press.*

"You're not going to write a *Baruch haShem* book, are you," she asked. *Baruch haShem* means "Thank God" and is a common expression in Orthodox parlance.

"What do you mean, a *Baruch haShem* book," I responded.

"You know. '*Baruch haShem,* I found Orthodoxy. *Baruch haShem,* my life straightened out, everything's terrific now, *Baruch haShem, Baruch haShem,* '" she explained.

The caller told me that she had converted to Judaism and only afterwards met and married an Orthodox Jew. After fourteen years of marriage he had decided to divorce her. Now her Orthodox Jewish friends were asking whether she would remain Jewish after the divorce.

"Fourteen years!" she said. "I didn't convert to marry him, I converted because I loved Judaism. What do they expect you to do?"

Many baalei teshuva have made the transition to Orthodoxy and have either never bumped up against the attitude I am describing or have chosen not to let it bother them. The baalei teshuva most comfortable in Orthodoxy may be those who dress, speak, and perhaps even think like Jews born Orthodox—those who have severed most of their ties with their previous, nonobservant way of life. Perhaps their mode of behavior does not constantly remind Jews born Orthodox of their secular past. For many people like my caller, though, Orthodox society may never have been outwardly hostile but also never trusted their commitment.

I could understand that my family and friends found it difficult to grasp why I was observant. As I have tried to explain, observant Judaism offers a life of constant, subtle pleasure centering around the general good feeling one can get from Doing the Right Thing, from doing what God wants. Most nonobservant Jews equate Orthodox Judaism with poverty, with ignorance, with sexism, with the "old country," or with the Holocaust. I could write a thousand pages and never convince many Jewish people that there is a shred of value to Orthodox Judaism. This book is not for them. But what of Orthodox Jews who appreciate Judaism for the same reasons I did? My family and friends were one thing, but I could not abide the fact that so many Orthodox Jews had no place in their hearts for people like me. Baalei teshuva live in a precarious position. Like it or not, they have burned at least some of their bridges behind them. They have cut themselves off, willingly or not, from some or all of their secular past. Some do so with a vengeance, but even those like me who try to balance an assimilated past with an observant present and future often find themselves caught between the two worlds. And that is the dilemma of baalei teshuva. The world they must leave behind cannot always understand why they became observant; the observant world they try to enter does not always want to offer them a place. In the kosher restaurant of life, baalei teshuva are the fried clams.

The film version of *The Chosen,* Chaim Potok's novel about two boys, one Orthodox and one Hasidic, opened just as I started law school. No less then twenty times did people ask me whether I had seen *The Chosen.* I could watch the thought pattern developing in their heads—a glance at my yarmulke, the connection to the film, the realization that here at last was something we had in common, and then the question, "Have you seen *The Chosen?*" At first it was funny, but I rapidly grew tired of the fact that people were associating me with religious Judaism and nothing else. "Hey," I wanted to say, "there is more to me—I like baseball and sunsets and a good meal and everything that everyone else likes." I was no longer Michael the person, I was Michael the Jew. Of course I was proud of my Jewishness; if I had not been proud, this whole business would never have started. But I was so self-conscious that I found it difficult to make many friends. I had always been gregarious—now I did not recognize my shy self. Uneasy lay the head that wore the yarmulke.

I stopped wearing it after the end of my first semester in law school. I cannot describe the relief I felt. I was still as exacting in my observance of the rest of Jewish law, but at least now it was private; I no longer felt "on display." This reminds me of another bit of irony. I was the most religious Jew that many of my friends and acquaintances had ever met, and with the exception of a few Orthodox cousins, I was the most observant person in my extended family. But to the Orthodox world, I was a child, barely versed in Talmud, barely experienced at keeping Jewish law. The Yiddish opposite of *frum,* "observant," is *frei,* the German word for "free"—not observant, free from the dictates of Jewish law. To put it simply, I was too *frei* for the *frum* and too *frum* for the *frei.*

I held my middle ground for two more years after the Poet O's Passover and my *Village Voice* blind date. That brings us to about four months ago, a gray, cold Friday afternoon in the

February of my second year of law school. (As I write it is the summer between my second and third years.) My frustrations continued to intensify. I was still something strange to my family and friends, and now, almost five years after the Twelve Days, I was still something strange to the Orthodox. Suddenly, something inside snapped.

That Friday afternoon I called an old girlfriend who lived in Northampton, Massachusetts. She was not home. Even after almost five full years, I knew few Orthodox people my age, and it was just too complicated to spend a Sabbath with my nonobservant friends—there was too much that was too difficult to explain, like why I could not go to a restaurant, or a movie, or even use an elevator. I needed more than anything to get out of New York and away from what had become the oppression of another Sabbath.

Traditional Judaism thrives on community, but I could not find that necessary community in New York, the center of the largest Jewish population in the world, and other baalei teshuva I have met suggest that I am hardly the only one to feel this way.

I borrowed a car and drove to Northampton. Every so often I pulled over and tried to telephone my friend; she was still not home. I continued into Northampton, arriving around five o'clock, not long before sundown, the first sundown on a Friday in about five years that would find me unprepared for Sabbath.

Elisabeth was at the restaurant in downtown Northampton where she worked as a waitress. Her shift began at six and ended at two in the morning. She was surprised, of course, to see me in Northampton without notice and in a restaurant anywhere on a Friday night. I quickly explained my situation and she gave me her keys, and I drove to a diner in nearby Florence, Massachusetts, where I had eaten regularly while in college.

I hear no angels weeping, I thought, as I drove a car on a Friday night for the first time in almost five years. I expected to hear angels weeping, I suppose, over my violation of the Sabbath.

No angels, I thought, as I stopped in a convenience store to buy a local newspaper to read over dinner. *I hear no angels weeping,* the strange, almost biblical-sounding thought forming and reforming itself in my mind, as I opened the door to the diner and hurriedly looked at each face, hoping that no one would recognize me. *No angels weeping* as I ordered dinner (broiled fish, squash, Coke; still no bacon cheeseburger). I heard no angels as I ate dinner and read the newspaper and paid the check and left a tip, all things that I had not done on a Friday night in almost five years.

No angels weeping as I drove to Elisabeth's apartment and let myself in and turned on the radio (Orthodox Jews do not turn on the radio during the Sabbath—what would the angels think of me now?) Several hours later Elisabeth returned.

"What's going on," she asked.

Elisabeth and I dated for almost a year in high school and then coincidentally went to the same college. Roslyn, where we grew up, is a predominantly Jewish suburb of New York City. Although Elisabeth was not Jewish (she had been raised a Quaker by her mother, whose family came from England), she knew enough about Judaism and about me to understand what I had been doing these last five years. I told her of my frustrations and how they had ended in my need that after-noon to get away.

"And now you're alone with a *shikse,*" she said with mock gravity, using the Yiddish word for "non-Jewish woman."

"You know too much," I laughed.

Elisabeth left me in her apartment and went to sleep next door at a friend's place. The next morning I took a bus to North Amherst to go to services at the Chabad House. I had not ridden a bus on a Saturday in almost five years—Orthodox Jews do not ride on the day of rest. The Sabbath is personified as the "Sabbath Queen" or "Sabbath Bride." Every Friday night, worshipers all over the world turn around at one point in the service to welcome her and bow to her. The idea of the "Sabbath Bride" is the only thing before which Jews bow, except for God Himself. As I rode that bus to Amherst I felt as though we were grinding the poor Sabbath Bride under our wheels.

I was almost ill with guilt. At the Chabad House the Derens and the others who knew me were quite surprised to see me— Orthodox people do not show up suddenly on Saturday mornings. I did not mention where I was staying or how I got there. That day, and over the next four months, I tried to figure out just where I stood in relation to Orthodox practice, and where I was headed.

"Maybe I'm going through a hormonal change," I wrote in my diary the following week. "Still in a quandary about religion—whether to remain Orthodox or not. I feel the strong need to reduce my commitment to observance, and I can't explain why. Maybe I'm tired of fighting."

And then three months later: "I have taken some giant steps away from Orthodoxy and I feel a bit odd about the whole thing. Part of the problem is [Orthodox] Jewish culture. There is a bias against baalei teshuva and I can't seem to get around it. I don't like being the subject of prejudice. It's a terrible feeling and I'm sick of it. I'm weary. I'm tired of fighting. I'm tired of being an outsider among my own people. I'm lost to Judaism, Orthodox people believe. Regardless of all I've done over the past five years. I've spent more of the past five years perfecting my Judaism than 95% of Jews. And what does it matter. 'Well, it's very nice. But would you want your daughter to marry one?'

"Bitter? You bet. But weary is the operative word. Maybe I'll get another burst of spiritual energy in a little while, in time for the holidays. But in the meantime, I must take time out."

And that is what I have been doing—taking time out, trying to reflect on the five years that brought me in touch with Orthodox Jewish religion, which I loved, and Orthodox Jewish society, where I did not seem to fit in. I have put my strict Orthodox practice, at least temporarily, in abeyance. Still no bacon cheeseburgers or fried clams, though—I have not gone all the way back, and I do not think I ever will. Although I am not fully observant as I write this, I still think of myself more as an Orthodox Jew than anything else. The Talmud teaches that "no man should be sure of himself until the day of his death," so I should refrain from announcing that I will conduct the rest of my life in one manner or another. At this point I should relate something that happened this summer.

Since this is the summer between my second and last year of law school, I am working as a clerk, or "summer associate," for a law firm located in Boston. Of the forty lawyers in the firm, at least three are observant to varying degrees. There was one attorney in particular who I felt certain was observant. Every other Thursday the firm holds a lunch seminar at which a partner or a client speaks about some aspect of the practice. The firm provides several trays of sandwiches, mostly cold cuts. I was not ready to eat nonkosher meat. Fortunately, there were a couple of egg salad sandwiches on a tray. I helped myself to one, and I waited to see who took the other one. Sure enough, it was the lawyer who I sensed was Orthodox. (He did not wear a yarmulke at the office, though.)

I mention the egg salad sandwiches because not long afterwards we had a conversation about the firm which turned, somehow, to the subject of religion.

"Do you know how I knew you were observant," I asked.

"How?"

"It was at the lunch seminar. You had an egg salad sandwich. Nobody has an egg salad sandwich unless they have to have an egg salad sandwich."

"That's right! And now that I think about it, you had an egg salad sandwich too! You know how I remember?"

"How," I asked.

"I ordered two sandwiches, and you took one of mine! You ate my egg salad sandwich!"

The Underground Railroad, the people that brought me Sabbath in Moscow, the Derens in Amherst, and the Roslyn Synagogue, had struck yet again. And this time it was at a corporate law firm, a place as far removed from Orthodox Judaism as any I could imagine. Somehow it always comes back to food, you say. But the kosher laws are an excellent metaphor for traditional Judaism—the idea that religion and morality should pervade all of the choices one makes in life, from the largest to the most trivial. And as long as we are talking about food, we might as well talk about fried clams.

Boston is one of the seafood capitals of the world, and fried clams are everywhere, but I never gave in to temptation. As I said at the outset, Orthodox Jews cannot relate to fried clams because they are inherently, biblically, irredeemably non-kosher. And yet, cheeseburgers (even those made from kosher meat and kosher cheese, which are nonkosher by virtue of the combination of milk and meat products) are a source of curiosity if not fascination to many observant Jews. Whether I return to Orthodoxy is of little concern to anyone but me, my God, and my family. The important question is the trend. Is there really no cure for assimilation? Do young Jews today stand as small a chance as I did of seeing something good in their heritage? Is there really no reason to think that Judaism means nothing more than chicken soup and Woody Allen (both of which are substantial contributions to Western culture, to be sure)?

And even if more young people are attracted to traditional Judaism, and even if they want the ability to unlock the secrets of those L-shaped blocks of Talmud text, and even if they want to experience the solidarity that I felt in places as disparate as Moscow, Brooklyn, and Amherst, Massachusetts; even if, somehow, every nonobservant Jew in the world suddenly "got religion," how would they react to an observant culture that does not always trust them?

I mentioned that some Orthodox Jews feel that secular Jews hide behind the "equal rites for women" issue in order to avoid an honest confrontation with traditional Judaism, and perhaps there is some truth to that belief. But non-Orthodox Jews rarely have an opportunity to learn about traditional Judaism. The associations of Orthodoxy with poverty, ignorance, sexism, and the Holocaust are hard to break down. Most nonobservant Jews, even ones with a deep interest in Judaism, do not even know how to go about studying their heritage.

One last issue. The term baal teshuva when applied to a secular Jew who has become Orthodox is, strictly speaking, inaccurate. A true baal teshuva is a Jew who grew up Orthodox, left the fold, and then returned in penitence—the Jewish prodigal son or daughter. The term is widely and mistakenly applied to Jews today like myself who knew nothing of Orthodoxy until relatively late in life. There is no word in Hebrew that adequately expresses the transformation from secular to religious life, and so baal teshuva is forced to fill the bill. (I have used that term throughout the book because it is really the only word we have; in Israel, baalei teshuva are called *chozrei b'teshuva*, which amounts to the same thing.)

It is no coincidence that there is no accurate term for baalei teshuva and that the position in the Orthodox community of those who do make the leap is often tenuous. Orthodox religions by nature move at glacial speed, and the "baal teshuva movement" is less than a generation old. Perhaps the passage of time and a greater influx of baalei teshuva into the Orthodox camp will make the transition easier. But what about today's baalei teshuva, who fit in with neither their own families nor their adopted communities?

Five years of experience in the Orthodox world lead me to conclude that mutual understanding is in short supply. Non-observant Jews owe it to their heritage, to all the Jews who believed that Judaism was too important to disappear, to investigate traditional Judaism, to ask questions and read books and try their hand, even for a few weeks, at keeping the Sabbath and kashrut. Orthodox Jews must sensitize themselves to the difficulties baalei teshuva face and must be aware of the self-doubt that plagues baalei teshuva for at least a short time during their metamorphoses—doubts that sometimes never leave.

Jews born Orthodox must abandon the idea that Jews born in nonobservant families are lost to Judaism, for that is a self-fulfilling prophecy. To return to my favorite metaphor, Jews born Orthodox must no longer view baalei teshuva as fried clams, as something foreign. Instead, they must think of baalei teshuva (and all Jews are potential baalei teshuva) as Jews just like themselves. If not, it will be goodbye, baalei teshuva, and not just goodbye, fried clams.

For Further Reading

I found these books helpful in my discovery of traditional Judaism, and I recommend them.

Berkovits, Eliezer, *Faith after the Holocaust*. New York: Ktav Publishing House, 1973.

Bleich, J. David, *Contemporary Halakhic Problems* (2 volumes). New York: Ktav Publishing House, 1977 and 1983.

Bunim, Irving, *Ethics from Sinai* (3 volumes). New York: Feldheim Books, 1964.

Heschel, A.J., *Between God and Man*, New York: The Free Press, 1959.

Horowitz, Edward, *How the Hebrew Language Grew*, New York: Ktav Publishing House, 1960.

Kitov, Eliyahu, *The Book of Our Heritage* (3 volumes). New York: Feldheim Books, 1978.

Lamm, Maurice, *The Jewish Way in Love and Marriage*. San Francisco: Harper & Row, 1982.

Lampel, Zvi, *Maimonides' Introduction to the Talmud*. New York: Judaica Press, 1979.

Oz, Amos, *In the Land of Israel*. New York: Vintage Books, 1983.

Rosner, Fred, and J. David Bleich, *Jewish Bioethics*. New York: Sanhedrin Press, 1979.

Sachar, Howard Morley, *A History of Israel*. New York: Knopf, 1979.

Schneerson, Menachem M., *On the Essence of Chassidus*, Brooklyn, N.Y.: Kehos, 1978.

Yezierska, Anzia, *Bread Givers*. New York: Persea Books, 1975.